Eve

The
Words
We Speak

Mary Drew

www.TenderFireBooks.com
Email: TenderFireBooks@gmail.com
Kevin C. Horton

"The Words We Speak" Copyright © 2018 by Mary Drew

For information contact;

North Shore Psychic Medium
Long Island, New York
Butterfly Blue Productions, Inc.
Email: mary.drew11@yahoo.com
Website: www.Marydrew.net
Manager: Lauren Wasserfall
wyngs24@aol.com
917-912-3433

Published by Tender Fire Books

ISBN: 978-1-7326927-0-1

First Edition: September, 2018

Dedicated to my four children:

Alex, Julia, John and Emerson

I love you… All I do… I do for you!

TABLE

OF

CONTENTS

Acknowledgements

In Memory of: John P. Scarola- My Brother- In pain and death comes rebirth and peace. *Forever My Butterfly*

Special Thanks

John and Teddie Scarola (My Parents): For always showing me I never walk alone. I am blessed to have you both.

Michael, Stephen, and Robert Scarola (My Brothers): My best friends. Your love and laughter is what feeds my heart.

Gina and Mary Rose: Thank you for being my friends.

Dorothy Drew: For giving me strength and advice. For always listening to me.

Lauren Wasserfall (My Manager and Ladybug): Thank you for believing in me!

My love, John Reed: For being my soul-mate, best friend, and angel. For teaching me that love is effortless and unconditional. You are my hero.

Johnny and Summer Reed: In my Heart you are my children and family!

The
Words
We Speak

Mary Drew

North Shore Psychic Medium

Long Island, New York

Butterfly Blue Productions, Inc.

REMEMBER

REUNITE

REJOICE

THE BIG GESTURE

I have been waiting all my life for this….

The Big Gesture!

You are probably wondering what this means.

Let me explain.

I had decided long ago, as early as I can remember that one day someone would show me what I call the Big Gesture. By my definition, these two words hold the greatest value toward my happiness. I wished that one day I would feel blessed to know an act of kindness and love so magnificent that it would humble me to my core.

It took forty years for me to figure out that the "Big Gesture" had already been made. I searched, waited, dreamed and prayed for it to come… all along never understanding that I already received my gift. I had spent my entire life performing random acts of kindness and delivering the BIG (and small) Gestures whenever and anywhere I could.

And finally, as simple as a breeze lifts a feather from its resting place, it hit me. The Big Gesture was received on March 17, 1972.

My Birthday!

God made "The Big Gesture" by sending me to the earth and giving me a chance at life. He was responsible for the start of my long spiritual journey, and has continued to send gestures to this very day. I am humbled by my realization and grateful for my beginning.

The words we speak and the gestures we make define us in so many ways. Together within this book, we will explore how common words and phrases create experiences so rich that they shape the people we become.

This story may be mine, and the words we discuss I have selected, but there is a lesson and a familiar path for everyone to explore. This book is just one of my "Many Big Gestures" in life. I hope you enjoy the journey and find peace and comfort within these pages. I write to you all from a happy, healthy, and balanced place in my life.

Your journey is just about to begin and within it I promise to show you how to give and receive big and small Gestures. No matter what topic I discuss or who reads this book, the message is always the same. Finding peace and comfort in your life, finding balance and acceptance, growing spiritually and mentally, reaching ahead toward love and away from hate is the only pot of gold we truly seek.

My Big Gesture…..

I
AM
NO
LONGER
A
PRISONER
TO
TIME.

Chapter 1

In Time

Life is never about Quantity, only the Quality of time spent here on earth!

In time you will understand. In time you will learn to cope. In time you will find love, happiness, and regain good health. How many times have I heard that? So many sentences and phrases and conversations begin and end with those two little words…
"In Time."

The words actually made me angry for a long time. I felt as though everything I wanted and desired could only be brought about with some lengthy calendar or clock counting my moments. I was tired of waiting for things to get better, to happen, to change. Tired and waiting are words we will definitely be looking at later on in our journey. For now, we are stuck within time… keeping track with little x marks across our calendar of life.

NOT ANY MORE!

I am no longer a prisoner of time. Want to know how I broke free? The change was actually quite simple. It all began with a thought and then a choice. While sitting on a train heading to New York City for my last dental appointment at my father's practice, it hit me. I had been living my life by a clock. Everything was being tracked by minutes, hours and days ahead. I was dwelling on my past experiences while at the same time trying to jump ahead to a steady and productive future. I organized my life by clocked moments and somehow ignored the most important time I actually wanted to focus on… The Present.

I think I have always been lost in time travel, jumping ahead with my thoughts and actions to satisfy my heart. I dwelled on past events and how I could learn from them to remove any margin for error in my life. I planned, shaped and filed my moments away into a future that may or may not come. As I sat on the train thinking, I came to see that the time I most wanted was right now…
In the moment. I wished for my life to be a series of wonderful acts of kindness to grow from. I wanted a life that I could appreciate and enjoy. I realized I needed to simply release myself from the place that I had boxed myself into.

And with that thought, I let it all go!

I left time on the train and watched as it released a steamy sigh of relief. As I walked from Penn Station and traveled up to the city streets, I felt myself leaving the dark tunnel below emerged as a changed person. It had always been my choice how to live my life and how to allow situations to affect me, yet somehow, I kept myself subservient to time. The rain hit my face as I stepped outside to the taxi stand, a symbolic baptism of my rebirth to a less stressful life. I knew I was still going to make decisions that impacted my future and family, however, I was just going to let my present moments build that path naturally.

I feel better having let go of my earthly clock. I now keep track of time in spiritual ways. I feel light. I feel free. I feel stronger than I ever have before.

Excited about my change and self-discovery, I shared my new found hope with a friend. Her reaction was supportive, but her understanding was followed by this comment: "Only time will tell if you can really change." I laughed at her play on words and said what only seemed as an appropriate response.

"In Time we shall see…"

I
AM
CONFIDENT
THAT LIFE
HAS
SO MUCH
TO
TEACH ME.

Chapter 2

Living in the Moment

We call it the Present because it is our Gift

So, here we are…. Living in the Moment. Well, I am. Are You?

I love this place I now call home. The present is my resting place. It brings me gifts of peace and joy, not fear and anxiety. I like living here without the restraints and pressures of where I am going and how I will get there.

Living in the moment has brought me down a wonderful road toward my mental, emotional and physical wellness. It has also delivered to me a better relationship with my spiritual side, my children's issues, and best of all, chased away the demons of my past.

My present state is full of unknowns and surprises and ironically I find that comforting. That does not mean that my entire life goes without errors and speed bumps. That would be silly not to mention completely unrealistic. I am human and like everyone else

I struggle with life-long issues. The gift that the present gives me is self-preservation and clear perception. I am learning to take care of my needs, slow down and view life from a very different angle.

I am actually going through a very difficult time in my life next to losing my brother many years ago. Experiencing the death of someone so close to you is extremely heart-wrenching and though cancer robbed John of precious years and events, that was just one kind of death I would come to learn to live with. Now, I mourn the loss of my marriage to divorce. This is a painful place where you learn to grieve the living not the dead. Like death, divorce brings out the "why" question. Why did this happen? Why did God hurt me like this? Why do things come to an end? All valid questions, but no matter what the answers were, I think I was just simply asking the questions in the wrong way. Why shouldn't this happen to me? It happens to millions of other people. Why would God try to hurt me, he loves me. Why not me? Living in the moment of this divorce and a new life-changing experience, has tested my strength and commitment to happiness. I am learning to live anew, start completely over, all while letting go of the red beast inside me. This is not an easy journey but essential for me to go through in order to reach an overall wellness within myself. I am confident that life has so much to teach me and that my present situation is going to empower my future. It is ok to struggle, feel sad, and even to be angry at times. It is teaching me to understand what I have lost and what I have yet to gain all at the same time. I am beginning to evolve, emerge, and emulate into a beautiful creature. However, there is something I must do first. I need to face my enemies and fears, and confront the monster in my closet...

Anger!

HAVE
WASTED
PRECIOUS
MOMENTS
LIVING
IN
ANGER.

Chapter 3

So Angry

Anger is the emotion that weakens our soul

It is impossible to count how many times we have felt anger. Each day we breathe brings happy thoughts and negative ones. We are constantly battling the emotions that anger brings forth. We struggle daily to overcome our fears and demons and release this fire from our existence. Most of us spend countless hours and years feeling angry. I should know… Anger has been the skeleton living in my closet since childhood. Let me tell you why.

Even as I write, I feel emotions swirling inside me. I am disappointed that I have wasted so much of my time living with this little red demon. If you asked most people who know me they would never think I battled anger. My friends and family tend to define me by positive words like kind, caring, friendly, strong, giving, and full of patience. If they only knew the truth! I live in a constant state of inner anger and turmoil. My every action is coated in fear, anxiety, and stress. Well… until recently that is! I have spent my entire life fighting with anger, and I have been losing most of the battles.

Here are just some of the things I feel anger toward: The death of my brother. The struggle to stay healthy and happy. The difficulties my children face in every aspect of their life. My divorce. My struggle to financially stay afloat. Just about every obstacle thrown my way.

I have fought hard against my anger, even felt held down by its power, but I have never "fully" surrendered myself to it. There have been times that I was not able to raise my head from my pillow and even cried myself to sleep. There have been times when only medication could calm my restless mind and ease my mental and emotional pain. I have been fighting all my life and this soldier has dodged many explosions.

It took my divorce and all the pain that it brought to the surface to finally let go of most of my anger. It has been a process and a journey, one that will take a lifetime to truly complete. However, I have taken the first step and won my first battle in this war. I am consciously making an effort to take down the cross that I have bared for so long. I am learning to forgive, have a greater level of faith, and most importantly, I am learning to let go. Giving my pain, fears, and insecurities up to God has allowed me to move forward. I am working on re-evaluating my life in a positive thankful way. Instead of focusing on my anger and all the things that have disappointed me, I am choosing to evaluate the aspects of my life that have been blessed with happiness. I can chose to focus on the negative or the positive, so I am taking door number two. I have spent so much of my life helping others move through their problems. I have also been raising four children and guiding them down a path of goodness. So, if I can help others, I must be capable of helping myself… right?

Ironically, I have accepted anger as a comfort place, my crutch to lean upon when life got too hard to handle. It was easier to stay angry at someone or a situation than to confront the parts of it that I did not like. It was easier to focus on all that had gone wrong instead of all that had gone right. My perspective on life became clouded by my fears and negativity. I was fatigued from my anger and saw no way out of it.

Then, the light bulb moment occurred. Well, ok… maybe it was a flicker.

What am I doing? I have wasted precious moments feeling sorry for myself or angry at the actions of others. I blamed everyone for making me feel bad, instead of taking responsibility for my feelings and actions.

It took my daughter, who was Twelve at the time, to make me realize that my anger was not just hurting me, but affecting my children as well. Here is what happened.

Julia and I sat in the kitchen together. I was busy making a call to my lawyer about the divorce while she worked on the couch doing homework. Julia is an extremely intelligent child but has way too much of me in her. She spends a great deal of her time living with anxiety and fears. I worry for her daily. She is an amazing kid, beautiful and caring, but she has regressed in her physical and emotional state over the past few years, and I realized that day it was all because of me. After I hung up the phone with the lawyer, discussing my frustrations with my living arrangement, Julia began to cry. Her tears quickly turned into a full blown anxiety attack. She struggled to breath and began to shake. I grabbed her tight, hugged her, and reassured Julia that all would be okay. I asked her what was wrong. This is what she said.

"Mom, I do not like this new you. You are angry and sad all the time. It makes me feel sad and confused. Will we be ok now that you and daddy do not love each other anymore?"

My heart broke in two and the pain I felt was so much worse than the pain of losing my marriage. I realized in my anger and sadness that my daughter was beginning to lose faith in me. My response was clear and swift.

"Julia. I love you. Your father loves you. We are blessed to have you and all the kids. But, it is true. Your mom has been stuck in a dark place. I wish I was stronger right now and did not show you this ugly side of me, but I am weak and tired from years of struggling. The good news is this… I can change! I will change!

Your love and support is helping me do that. I will let my anger go. I promise."

The words escaped my lips and with it the truth. I would let it all go for the sake and well-being of my children. I would have to learn new coping skills and find the best way to express my feelings without building fear or sadness within my four babies. I love my children, they are my life and greatest source of happiness. It is through their presence that I let anger go.

It was best decision I could have ever made. Not just for my children, but for myself! I feel satisfied and at ease. I feel as if the cross that I have struggled to carry upon my back has been burned to ash. I believe again in the positive and see only possibility in my life. My back hit the wall and I came out swinging. I am a step ahead of the game in this journey because I am learning to release my anger. I waited a long time to reach this point. My wait was difficult and frustrating, but that is now a thing of the past. I am running toward my dreams.

This is just the exercise my soul needed!

SLOW DOWN AND APPRECIATE THE BIG AND SMALL GESTURES OF LIFE.

Chapter 4

Wait one minute!

Waiting is just another word for patience

"Wait one Minute!" I yell from the bathroom. Never a minute alone I laugh to myself. It is a miracle that I use the bathroom at all most days. The kids are constantly on top of me, making demands, asking for my help with homework or showers. I barely get a minute to myself. While going through the divorce, I realized I needed a career after being a stay-at-home mom all these years. So I enrolled in on-line school and got my degree in Landscaping. I started my own business and took time to develop that. I also have other talents and degrees that bring forth an income. I am somewhat of a jack of all trades kind of girl. However, work has been sitting on the back burner because I need to focus on the well-being of my children. The divorce has taken a toll on them, and my job as a stay-at-home mom was critical, now more than ever!

Now, lets' talk about the word Wait. It is actually a strong and powerful word that is wrapped in patience and growth. There is so much to be learned through waiting for your life to progress. Waiting has taught me that sometimes the focus needs to come off of myself and put toward others. Being a mother of four you learn early on that waiting and patience goes hand in hand. I spent countless hours waiting for a house to get clean, kids to listen to me, standing on long lines at a store with children in tow, and waiting for my personal life to be lived. Any mother or father understands that waiting is not just hard for children, grown-ups too struggle with waiting.

As we get older, we find it hard to be patient. Once again time comes into play, and we feel we do not have the time to wait. We are busy, fast-past, moving individuals living in a society where everything is accessed quickly through the touch of a button. We can shop from our cell phones, pay bills online, and go through a drive through window to get our morning coffee. We are being conditioned not to wait; not to hold onto the virtue of patience. Worst of all this is the generation our kids are growing up in. They no longer have to wait for anything or appreciate the art of learning something slowly and perfecting that skill. Even the words we speak and write are changing. We abbreviate words all the time now through texts and have moved away from the skill of rhetoric and writing.

No wonder why our kids have no patience to wait for their dinner to be cooked or for a friend to reply to a text they sent one minute earlier. If we do not slow down and relearn patience, we will miss out on so much that life has to teach us. We are forgetting what it is to enjoy the simple pleasures.

I can actually recall times that I have driven to and from a location without a real conscious memory of doing it. It was as if I put myself on cruise control and just moved through the motions, without feeling or observing what was happening in that moment. We do it all the time.

I have made an effort to slow down and appreciate the little and big gestures that life has to offer. I relish in the moments when I see my children laughing, studying the directions the lines go on their face as a smile breaks free. I point out beautiful skylines and starry nights to my children on car drives. I am experiencing life again.

My kids still do not like to wait for things but they are learning over time that it can be pleasant and not painful. I purposely get on long lines at stores just to remind myself that waiting is good. Most of the time I spend waiting opens the door to meeting new people, learning new things, and finding out that life is so worth waiting for.

While finding my life through this divorce and learning how to be financially independent, waiting has served me well. Expanding and extending the time I need to process feelings or complete tasks, has opened great doors for me. I am actually where I need to be at this time. I am happy to wait for new moments to come because waiting shows me the possibility that there are moments yet to be explored. There is something so exciting and risky in not knowing what will come next or when it will arrive. There is a rush of life building within me that gives me energy to see what tomorrow will bring.

However, waiting does not mean you are being let off the hook. I am not giving you permission to sit back and wait for things to happen or come to you. It is actually the opposite that I want you to do.

I am imploring you to go out and live life… Not remain still within it. Life happens because all we do in our present state defines future events. We need to make our dreams and goals become a reality. If we are longing to find love, than we must go out and seek it. We must be patient that our hard work and effort will bring to light the answers we seek. Once we put ourselves out in the world we can wait to see what effects come from our actions and commitment to living.

I urge you, next time you go to the store, get on the longest checkout line you can find, then give yourself time to view what is around you, notice people, textures, and conversations. Take the "wait" moment and reflect upon your day or the things you would like to see manifest in your life. Test your patience and see what miracles can emerge from within.

FIND THE GOOD IN THE BAD IN ALL SITUATIONS.

Chapter 5

This Too Shall Pass

All that is meant to be will unfold before your very eyes

I think this saying is my mother's favorite one… "This too shall pass!" She has spoken these words repeatedly since I was a young girl.

Now that I am grown, I find myself repeating that same phrase all the time to friends, family and clients of mine. I have definitely said it to at least ten different mother's on the playground when their children were crying or misbehaving. My friends have said it to me during the real down points of my life, especially during the tantrum years of my two daughters.

"This too shall pass." What does that really mean anyway? What will pass? It is actually a phrase from the bible, a proverb indicating that all material conditions, positive or negative, are temporary. Since I am a practicing Catholic, this makes sense to me. I base a great deal of my strength in life to my faith in God and angels. I have always believed in finding the good in all bad situations. That is not always easy to do, considering depression from our struggles can warp our view on what is positive in the hard times of our life. It takes skill and a fighting spirit to force one's self to always look at the bright side of a situation.

I actually use a cheat sheet for this attitude in life. The reason I can be confident with my life or the worst parts of it is because of my relationship with angels and Spirit. For those of you who do not know me, I am known as the North Shore Psychic/Medium. Yes, I see dead people!

My ability to see, feel, and hear people who have passed on or see angels from time to time, is a gift that I have been blessed with since the age of ten. I love this ability and do not fear it by any means. I find it quite natural to me and have made it a normal part of my life and my children's lives. They know exactly what I do and find comfort in our talks of heaven and spirits. It is our faith that has built a strong foundation for us to walk upon. But for me, it is my rare gift that has driven my true fears away and helped me cope with life problems. There is no greater fear or problem than the thought of illness or death. I have experienced plenty of illness and seen what disasters death leaves behind.

So, any problem outside of death and illness, well they are simply removable objects blocking our path toward peace and wellness. The best part about our problems is these situations do pass, just like the Bible states. Just like the saying my mom reiterates. All problems can be repaired even the worst ones. Sometimes we correct them all on our own, and other times, it takes the input of an entire family or community.

As a Psychic/Medium it is my job to bring peace, sometimes closure and acceptance to a part of life that appears unacceptable… death. No one wants to forgive death for what it has stolen. I tell clients all the time who struggle to cope with the loss of someone dear to them, that grieving is forever. In the area of death and grieving, this is the one place that we accept time as our friend not foe. Time heals all wounds or allows us to get use to wearing our brand new scars. Most scars are not left within or upon us to constantly be reminders of our pain. I think our scars (emotional or physical) are more like badges of honor. We need to wear them proudly to remind ourselves we are not just surviving our ordeal or hurtful experience, but we are continuing to live life through it.

No matter what you may be facing at the moment, you can rest assure that absolutely the pain associated with the event will pass. Strength and love will get us through the worst of things. Take a minute now and reflect upon just one terrible moment in your life. Remember how you felt. Remember how dark those days seemed. Now, fast forward your memory back to today. Are you still dealing with that problem? Have you forgotten or moved passed it? Are you happy, relieved, and smarter for experiencing it? That too did pass… and here you are… Living.

You made it here because you believed in seeking the light at the end of that problems tunnel. What probably guided you through the darkness were feelings of hope, faith, and forgiveness. Hope and faith make sense, right?

Forgiveness is always the last part of healing or getting past a hardship. Half the time we spend forgiving it is toward another, but the other half is forgiving ourselves. Hardest thing we will ever need to learn to do.

We will look at forgiveness closely because it is crucial for our soul's constant nourishment.

I will explain how forgiveness has taken me so far past my pain and problems, that all I see now are specs of their existence.

I am in a good place and I would love some company here.

Will you join me?

FORGIVE YOURSELF AND OTHERS FOR THE PAIN IN YOUR HEART.

Chapter 6

Forgive me!

I will forgive you, but I won't forget you.

Hands down the worst advice I have ever given anyone or myself...

"Forgive but never forget."

Well... I was wrong and withdraw my statement forever. I now see that forgiveness is letting go and forgetting what we have done to ourselves or others. Forgiveness is actually what it has been defined to be. Letting those who have hurt us be released from the anger we hold for them. We think that by holding our hatred, or hurt over them that suddenly, the person will feel remorse and sorrow. That our betrayer will run back to us begging to be forgiven because they just can't sleep at night knowing the pain they caused us.

The people who usually hurt us have a life-long pattern of hurting those around them. And to read your mind and answer your question… these people feel just fine and sleep like babies. There are different types of pain, different types of people and so, with that comes different levels of forgiveness. Let me explain.

Forgiving the Enemy: Part one

What does it mean to forgive our enemy? Enemies are people who fight hard against us; who try desperately to take us down. Sometimes they are friends. Sometimes they are people within our family. And sometimes it is people we know within our community or society. I have met someone who falls into all these categories in my life at some point or another. Most of these people are negative blood-sucking vampires who intend to drain the life out of others. Some are people who are so angry at their own lives that they can only project more anger and sadness. And some are just products of their environment – people acting and reacting to situations based on the principles of how they were raised and what they were taught. All these people share one thing in common: They are lost individuals. So, what are we to do then? How do we avoid these people, stay clear of their storm, or find the strength to forgive them when we are wronged?

"If you lay down for someone, they will always walk all over you."

We can spend endless hours fighting against these people or trying to make sense of the pain they brought to our lives. But, it takes real courage to find what role we took in all this and if we will take any responsibility for what has just occurred. Most people cannot bring forth pain unless you allow yourself to feel pain. Most people cannot drain the life from you unless you have already tilted your head and exposed your neck.

I have spent years venting to friends and blaming others for the pain they brought to my life. I can recall a time when I allowed a friend to take great advantage of my kindness again and again. I made a choice to take some time away from this friend and re-evaluate her behavior and my role in allowing her to depend on me so severely that she no longer could cope on her own. I confronted her asking for space during the loss of my marriage trying to redirect my focus off of her and back to my kids and my health. She verbally attacked me and did her best to try and take me down. She threatened my life, my family, and my future. Most of her words were spoken in the heat of her anger; I am sure she does not even remember all she said. The bad thing was I kept all her hate texts and burned the image of those words in my brain. I allowed it to sink in, corrupt my positive soul, and let hatred and anger begin to grow there. I spent months hating her, reliving in my mind all I didn't do to deserve such betrayal. But as the days turned into months and the months shaped half a year, I realized she could care less for the pain she caused. It was not her who was losing sleep... it was me. She did not know compassion or forgiveness, yet ironically, she came from a loving mother and amazing family. There was a darkness within her that tortured others, but worst of all herself. I began to analyze her behavior using my own psychological experiences, and realized anger toward her was wasted energy. If anything, I should have been praying for her all along. In the end, I feel sorry for this person. She is void of remorse and regret and destined to forever repeat her mistakes. I decided to let the anger go, as I have done from my divorce, and with that decision came peace and forgiveness. I forgive her, or anyone for that matter who has ever hurt or broken me. I take responsibility for the fact that I allowed these people to take advantage of me, which brings me to the second part of Forgiveness in this chapter.

Forgiving Ourselves: Part 2

It is also one of the hardest things to do. Most of us have secured a weight at the end of our forgiveness chain. I call that weight guilt.

I have spent my whole marriage and divorce feeling guilty. I was guilty for not doing more for my children even after I had given them all I could that day. Guilty for not cleaning enough, feeling tired or sick, sitting down, wanting a break after spending months without one. I was guilty for loving so much that I made myself vulnerable to the pain of being ignored. I felt guilty for my marriage ending because the choice to stay in the emptiness hurt more. I felt guilty for disappointing my children, making them a statistic, and bruising their tender souls. I even felt guilty for cursing a man who clearly was not meant for me, and hating him for so long. I felt guilty for venting to others about my pain and burdening their lives. I felt guilty for so many things and struggled every day to forgive myself for not being stronger.

In order for me to attain peace, fullness and happiness, I knew I had to find a way to forgive myself for everything. It was crucial for my self-preservation. If I didn't forgive me, then how could I find the strength to forgive anyone? I didn't want to snowball out of control or fall so far down that picking myself up would appear impossible. I wanted to be a good role model, so my kids could look up to me and so I could be proud of myself.

As a religion teacher, I began to review my job as a catechist and Catholic. I preached to my class about gratitude, compassion, forgiveness and acceptance. I taught them what it was like to be a Good Samaritan and follow the path that Jesus paved so graciously for us. I listened to Father Bob the pastor at my church, give homily after homily about God's plan for us. So, I did what anyone in my shoes would do… dropped the pity party I was having and opened my heart to God's lessons. It was on my journey back to faith that I met self-forgiveness.

We all know that forgiving ourselves is like taking out the garbage… we just don't want to do it. It takes effort and a full-time commitment to one's self. Most of us are so busy taking care of children or spouses that we just do not know how to focus on ourselves. We grow sick and tired of having to juggle so many jobs in our day and then to top it off we have to focus on healing our soul too.

Just like we make commitments to our jobs, raising our children, or exercising and eating well, we too must show our dedication to our spirit. We need to move to a place free from guilt and the burden it brings.

So, let's make a deal. Start today. Forgive yourself for one small thing.

Release the guilt.

Embrace the idea that life would flow lighter and gentler if the wave that carried you was pushed forward by a forgiving gust of wind.

DO NOT DISTURB ME - CAN'T YOU SEE I AM HEALING HERE?!

Chapter 7

Sick and Tired

"Zzzzzzzzzzzzzzzzzzzzzzzzzzzzzzz"

Oh, where to begin!

If I had a dollar for every time I started a sentence with the phrase, "I am sick and tired of..."

God knows I'd be a rich woman.

Unfortunately, I never found money at the end of that phrase. Truly it was the complete opposite. I grew poor in spirit and in physical health. Stating that I felt sick and tired all the time took a toll on me; it made me actually sick and tired.

Tell me if this sounds familiar to you:

"I am sick and tired of no one appreciating me around here."

"I am sick and tired of nothing going my way."

"I am sick and tired of no one listening to me."

"I am sick and tired of feeling alone, lonely, depressed and sad."

"I am sick and tired of never having money."

"I am sick and tired of feeling sick and tired!"

"Welcome to Club Pity Party!"

As my ex-husband would comically say… "Would you like some cheese with that wine?"

We spend at least eighty percent of our day complaining about the things that aggravate us and fatigue us mentally, emotionally, and in the end physically. We may have many valid reasons to complain. We even have the right to bitch and moan if our day has been hard. We are entitled to our right to feel frustrated, put out, or simply just done. We legitimately feel exhausted from our struggles and problems. So why shouldn't we complain? I'll tell you why: We all know what stress is. Some of us even know first-hand what it can do over time. Stress can kill you or make you sick. I should know. Here is what happened.

My stress in life started long before marriage and a divorce. I have been friends with stress since my early teenage years. We were actually best friends until recently. You know the saying… Who needs an enemy when you have a friend like this? Well, that saying truly applies here. Stress was next to me every step of the way. When I took a math test, stress was there. When I was dumped by a boyfriend, stress was there. When I job hunted, got married, and started raising my children, stress held my hand.

I eventually out grew stress and kicked it to the curb, but unfortunately, I waited too long and carry the scars it left behind. Some of my scars are noticeable and some lay deep within my heart and mind. I guess it doesn't matter where the scars ended up, because they are permanent. I was determined not to attain anymore battle wounds, so I released stress one very cold winter day. I will tell you all about it, but first let me explain how stress made me sick.

Stress always made my immune system weak so I spent much of my life sick with varying illness. Colds, flu, stomach issues, and anxiety attacks were just some of the little viruses it brought to my world. The more I worried the weaker I became; the more I worried the stronger stress became. I knew it laughed at my difficulties and enjoyed the pain it bestowed upon me. Yet, for some reason I am not quite sure of, I allowed it to live close to me.

Just like so many days in my life, I woke one morning fatigued and depressed. All four of my children were home sick with a stomach virus. It was a typical routine here… forever a prisoner to my house and sick kids. I was angry. Mostly, I was just simply sick and tired. I felt my stress building as the phone rang early that morning. I grabbed it to only be greeted with a soft and gentle voice. It was one of my very dear friends from my community. Her voice cracked as she began to speak, "Mary, do not turn on the television, I know you will get upset, but listen to me, many children and teachers were shot and killed this morning at a school. It's horrible. I want to go and get my kids from their school; I am worried they are not safe."

My heart ached from the news and my thoughts immediately went to the parents of all the children who had died. I quickly gathered my thoughts in order to say something comforting to my friend. Instead of insisting that her children were safe and she had nothing to fear, it dawned on me that I was speaking to another mother of four children. So, I said what felt right, "Go get your children and bring them home. Hug them and kiss them."

What else could I say at a time like this? Remember, my kids were already home sick, so they were in my care. I knew they were safe. I did as my friend instructed and did not watch the television. I walked to my bedroom and opened the window to catch my breath. The cool air blew in and its breath was coated with a burning hickory wood smell. I felt my shoulders lower and found myself lost in a daydream. Remembering my brother John and the many cozy fires we built together at our parent's house. Oh how I missed him. I replayed the image of my parent's first embrace after he died, and the thought made me shiver all over. How would these parents go on? I prayed quietly in my room. You all are probably thinking I sat and prayed for the families who lost all those children. Well… that is partly right.

Selfishly, I also prayed for myself. I was ashamed of the person I was at this time. I was the opposite of the mother I had been prior to the divorce. I was angry and snapped at the children a great deal of the time. I was annoyed and put out by their everyday demands and sickness. I was so ashamed that I prayed for strength. I prayed for my happiness and that of my children's happiness. I prayed for good health for us all and stronger times ahead. Most of all, I prayed for God to end my friendship with stress because I no longer liked the influence it had over me. Stress did not kill me, but it came close many times.

How could I place so much importance on all the things that held me down, instead of the four things that held me up? My kids were once again the best reason for luring stress out of my life and kicking its big fat butt to the curb.

And it was on that tragic day in so many people's lives, that I gave my problems and worries up to God. With all the despair and sadness in the world, how could I place so much importance on the little things that blocked my path? I was working on eating right and exercising at that time, so I was already fighting back consciously. I was putting in motion plans to financially support my life. I was finding love during one of the most hopeless times of my life. I was fighting back at stress and winning without even realizing it. However, in order for me to continue to progress I needed to send a hard right hook to stress for the knockout punch. It was time to remove it from my life for good. With God's blessing and faith in me, I knew I could do this.

This doesn't mean that from time to time stress won't come knocking at my door looking for a rematch. In fact, it already has. I just choose not to answer the door anymore. I am in search of peace and love from here on out, so there is no room for stress in my life.

I am hanging a "Do Not Disturb" sign on my door from now on. Stress will be lurking around every corner, but this time I will be ready.

TAKE
RESPONSIBILITY
FOR
THE PARTS
OF LIFE
YOU
DO NOT
LIKE
AND MAKE
A
CHANGE!

Chapter 8

Take Responsibility

So the time has come to act like a grown up... ready, set, go!

The time in my life has come for me to grow up and start acting like an adult. I guess I have actually been doing that all these years, especially as a mother. I have done all I can for my children and the people in my life.

However, I did make a mistake. I wronged someone I cherish, in a terrible way, that person was me!

I neglected my needs on every level. My emotional side was placed on the back burner. My mental needs were ignored and exhausted. My physical state was run down and breaking apart. I did right by so many, but failed in the most important role I could take on. My needs were not being met, but I made a choice to sacrifice myself for my children. I played the role of a martyr and could have won an Emmy for my performance.

It was time to take responsibility for myself without letting go of my duties as a mother or friend. I needed to find the most important thing to allow this to happen… Balance. Without balance in my life I would constantly fall to one side or another, never giving myself the chance to juggle it all with ease and comfort. I needed to re-invent myself and create a life that was not just for my children to enjoy but for me to enjoy as well.

I realize that while trying to make this change, this would actually be the hardest part of my life. Letting go of anger, finding forgiveness, and reducing stress is something we can all learn to do. Practice makes perfect as we all know. Balance, managing all the above and every other role you play in your life is a whole other story. Finding my balance has taken me a great deal of time and I am still searching for the best way to do that. Sometimes, what works for me one week, needs to be altered and revised for the next. So instead of focusing on the big picture, I have been taking smaller steps toward success. I try to focus on the day, and creating a stable environment and structure for those twenty-four hours. I keep things simple and try not to over complicate my situation with obsessive compulsive thoughts. I strive to make the day balanced through organization and patience with the small strides I am making.

I need to focus some of the attention back on myself not because I am selfish or ignore the needs of others, but simply because without a well-rounded life, I am just no good to anyone else. How can I do all that I do, be there for all the people I am there for, if I am just a shell of a person? It is time to take advantage of the fact that I am capable and strong and able to handle even more than I originally thought I could.

God never gives me, or anyone, more than they can handle. It is obvious through my many life experiences that God has a great deal of faith in me and believes I can multi-task and adapt to all kinds of change and stress. I am starting to see that by taking full responsibility for my needs is going to instill within me a wonderful sense of ownership and accomplishment.

I need to adjust the focus back to me in order to rebuild my confidence and self-esteem. I lost both those traits long ago during the years I was married. I became hollow and worn. Raising four children and all they battle took so much out of me. Living without love and a soul-mate depressed and weakened my emotional state. Life was hard. I may have been busy, never without a minute alone and constantly on the go, but in a realm where I was never alone, I felt lonely and isolated. The schedule of my life separated me from friends, personal dreams, and the world. I may have been living and performing tasks in the eyes of those around me, but ironically, my life resembled the movie starring Bill Murray, Groundhog Day. It was as if I was stuck in the same day destined to continuously repeat itself. There was no difference between the days of the week and the weekends. My life was a series of chores, caring for children, and more chores. I felt unsatisfied and disappointed.

I love being a mom, do not misunderstand me, but I felt there was so much more to me that was not being shown. What I missed most of all was having what all women want… a partner, a lover, a friend, and a soul-mate. I lost myself, most of all, in the role of wife. I wanted to be appreciated, desired, cherished and loved by my husband. I wanted the white picket fence lifestyle, but that was just not so. After the marriage ended, I felt relieved and disappointed all at the same time. It was hard to accept that at the age of 39, I would have to begin again, find myself, care for my children, and wonder if my future would ever hold love.

Here I was, divorced at the middle of my life. If someone was to date me, he would have to be an angel, sent from above to take on so much. I do not come alone, I am a package deal. So, I came to the understanding that I would have to be patient and hope that love was out there. In the meantime, I would focus on the children, adjusting them to their new world. I would also focus on me. Changing all the traits I felt were weak and needing to be replaced. I would set my sights on my goals and try to establish myself financially. I had a lot of work ahead of me and I knew it wouldn't be easy. I would always keep in the back of my mind the hope that when the time was right I would receive a sign, a gesture from God that love was on its way.

Chapter 9

I Love You!

There is nothing I'll ever want more than another year of you!

The sweetest card I ever received contained the words written above. True love! Does it exist?

ABSOLUTELY!!!!

To my surprise love came during a time of my life that seemed hopeless and grim. Believe me, the last thing I was looking to find was anything that could confuse or complicate my life during my divorce. I already had so much on my plate and could not begin to feel good in a place where my heart felt empty and torn. I actually believed while living through my divorce that no man would want or love a woman so broken and lost.

I spent many nights crying alone while the children slept

and prayed to my brother John in heaven to send me his strength and a sign. On occasion, I would meet up with friends to take my mind off all the worry.

We all know at my age the bar scene can get old real fast. Almost all the men who approached me to convince me how great they were, had more bones in their closet than I cared to see. By nights end, conversations turned into cheap pick-up lines, sexual advances, and as every drop of alcohol absorbed into their brains, the true stories arose of how they still had girlfriends or wives even when they claimed at first they didn't. I was appalled by the lack of honesty, the thought of me being someone's side piece, and how fast a man could run after hearing I was a mother of four.

My friends and I always had laughs, but that was not the life I was looking to enter in on the coat-tail of a divorce. If I was to ever meet someone, date again, it would have to be worth it for myself but also right for my children. Any person going through a divorce can go out and have fun keeping separate their personal life from their children's lives. Going out all the time and leaving my children home with sitters or grandma's was NOT the thing to do during the divorce. They needed me and I needed to be home as much as possible.

It is great to know what you need to do and when you need to do it, but you cannot stop love from coming if it is sent from heaven. That is definitely where mine came from!

I met the love of my life while going through my divorce. A dear friend of mine from childhood has a daughter who is ill. He and his wife continuously hold fundraisers for her. I am not going to mention their names or their daughter's illness to keep their private life private. What is important to know is that even in their difficult times, they continued to do good things and even think about all I was going through.

A decision was made by my friend to introduce me to my love, John. Ironically, he shares the same name as my deceased brother. A common name yet so special to me. As a psychic/ medium I love to point out to people things that are considered supernatural, unusual, or special about a circumstance or person.

It is through the fine details of a reading with me that the client comes to understand how solid and valid my abilities are. Many readings contain information about shared events in the lives of those living and dead. For example, my daughter Emerson is born on April 27th, the same birthday as my Uncle Bernie who is passed. Another example is my Son Alex who was born on February 7th. He unfortunately shares his birthday with the death day of his Uncle John, not my brother John, his father's brother also passed. Like I said, the name John is special.

When I met "My John" we spent a great deal of time getting to know one another by phone. It was strange to talk to another man while dealing with the divorce but I enjoyed our conversations. During one of our phone calls I asked a normal question and inquired when his birthday was. He responded with the date June 11th. At that moment I knew my brother was sending me a sign from heaven. You see, my brother John passed away on June 11th. And though many see this as a sad day or a day to forget, I see it as his new birthday. So instead of mourning John on that day, I celebrate with my kids with a cake and balloons. I tell them stories every year on that day about my brother. I explain how June 11th was his rebirth into a new life with God. I do not want them to be sad nor do I want to remember my brother with tears and pain. I chose to remember his life with laughter and the many smiles he brought to my world.

So, the two John's share an event… a day… the best day. I was excited to meet this man and hoped we would hit it off in person. I had no idea what was in store and will never forget the moment I first saw him. Is it possible for someone to lose their breath and have their heart race faster than ever before all at the same time? That is exactly what happened to me!

For someone who always has a lot to say and is usually never at a loss for words, I became mute and nervous. So cliché, but our eyes met from across a crowded dance floor and suddenly the world slowed down around us. I do not remember anything else in that room except the image of John walking toward me. If a man could be described as stunning or beautiful than those are the only two words that come to mind. We spoke for hours, and I held on to every word that rolled off his tongue as if it were his last. He had charm and an air of confidence about him. As he moved from conversation to conversation with me or those around us, he shifted position with such ease. I was in love. I barely knew this man. I was trapped in a depressing divorce, yet all I could see were stars. I was in my own movie of sorts, a romantic novel if you will, and I was eager to turn the page in this story.

What happened next was just shy of a fairytale. The words that came to me through verbal communication or text were phrases I had never heard before. The outpouring of love and support was incredible. We shared our stories of life, talked about our children, and as each word passed I fell deeper in love.

Love came to me at a time in my life when I honestly believed it didn't exist. I had no way of knowing where this relationship was going but I took a great leap of faith. I was not going to date him just because I was lonely. I would rather be alone for the right reasons than stay with someone just because I was afraid. He was special… It felt right, from the start.

Amazing love… beautiful and kind … a man I never want to live without. I am beyond blessed. John gave me confidence in myself, supported my dreams and visions, and best of all, concentrated on my strengths not my weaknesses. He listened and understood yet never told me how to make decisions or what to do. I appreciate, not just the love, but the friendship we have developed. He really is my soul-mate.

So, why do I tell you all this? This chapter is written for all the people out there who are going through a hard time or just feel alone. This chapter is the notion of hope delivered to you all on paper. No matter how bad things are or how dark the world can appear, there is always another chance. Now, go out there and create something meaningful.

I
THINK
I
CAN!
I
THINK
I
CAN!

Chapter 10

I Can't!

"I may not have gone where I intended to go, but I think I have ended up where I needed to be."
— Douglas Adams

       Best quote I ever read was the one written above, by Douglas Adams. I absolutely have not gone to many of the places I planned on going, yet no matter what path I took and where I ended up, an amazing lesson was always right behind me.

       I realized throughout my journey that the focus was always on the future and my present mental state was holding me back. I became fixated on The, "I Can't," theory. You all know what that theory states even if you never really took the time to think about it before now. The theory of, "I Can't," is exactly what those two small words mean. I can't do anything right. I can't be there for everyone. I can't see past tomorrow. I can't do this! Do those words sound familiar to you?

I truly believed no matter how capable I was, how smart I might be, how well I could multi-task, that there was no real way to do it all and succeed. My "I can't" philosophy was my hearts way of telling my brain I did not believe I could do what I set out to do. I was afraid of each event and every outcome. I was afraid to fail. I did not want to disappoint myself, but that was not the true fear that held me back from doing something or trying. My real fear came from failing my kids. I wanted to always be there for them and remain a good role model, but how could I do that and juggle becoming financially stable? Divorce changes you in so many ways. For me, it brought the greatest fear to light I am alone and need to step away from the role of stay-at-home mom into working mom. How?

I refused to lessen my role as a mother. So, in that mindset, I became handicapped with setbacks and the "I can't" attitude. So as days passed by, I found my life struggles difficult to manage or balance and had no fool proof plan for how to change things. Something needed to change. Was it my outlook on life? Did I need someone to come in and rescue me? Maybe, what I really wanted was the wrenches to stop being thrown into my machine called life and halting its rotation. I did not have the answers and looked to anyone around me for guidance and suggestions. I studied people and how other families lived. I asked friends and family members how they juggled the activities in their lives. I read countless self-help books and used my escape in prayer to help clear my mind and open it to fresh ideas. I tried everything I could.

I was lost. I could not find my way around this problem. What problem you ask? My dilemma: juggling four young kids and working full time to support them. I needed to drive them to school and pick them up each day. I needed to be home after school to care for them, cook, complete homework, clean, and put them to bed. Finding a job that is flexible with hours, has no evening or weekend schedules attached to it, and allows for sick kids home and time off, well, you guessed it.... nearly impossible I needed answers and I needed them quick!

The most perfect dream came to me one night and with it my answer. Every place I sought an answer from was met with a brick wall. One night while sleeping my mind drifted off to a calmer place, a forest lined with trees standing tall on a bed of leaves. It was in the middle of this dreamy place that I met my brother John. He looked so relaxed with his back to the ground staring up at the canopy of braches. He did not speak to me; he just waved me over and patted the ground a few times. Excited, I ran over to hug him and lay down next to him. I noticed the ground beneath me was hard and cold and carpeted in the colors brown and black. The leaves were not bright and vibrant and worry settled in my chest. Where was I and why was my brother in such a gloomy place? I asked John how he found this forest and what he was doing there. He pulled his left arm from behind his head and pointed up to the sky. I followed the straight path his arm formed and brought my eyes upward to the direction of the sky through the web of branches. I could see that past all the brown and black rotting trees and clutter was something beautiful. I remember sighing in the dream but not out of relief that my brother was near but frustration instead. John could sense my sadness, and finally spoke to me. Here is what he said:

"Do you see the blue sky out there? Glance between the branches and you will see it. You cannot go around the trees to see it. There is always another tree standing in this forest. If you want to get to the sky you have to look up and go through the branches. Do it with your eyes. Do it in your mind. Can you picture the whole sky past the branches? If you can do that, then you can fix all the things wrong in your life. You asked me to come, so here I am. We are at the bottom together. Now you must go up and out alone. I will watch you the whole way to make sure you get there. If you look back you won't see me anymore but I will be close by."

I jolted out of my dream feeling very clear. The visit from my brother did not make me sad or miss him more. It gave me energy and peace. This is the first time I am speaking of this dream to anyone. I did not share it with my family or friends because I felt it was an intimate moment between my brother and myself. I wanted to savor that feeling and wait until the time was right to share it with others. That time is now. I needed time to reflect upon the dream and what it was that John was trying to tell me. I kind of felt there could be many ways to view this dream or interpret it. I was unsure and needed something to piece it all together.

March 18, 2013, just one day after my forty-first birthday, I found the missing piece to my message from John and with it the meaning to the dream.

"Promise me you'll always remember: You're braver than you believe, and stronger than you seem, and smarter than you think." Christopher Robin to Pooh. A. A. Milne Words in a book found buried for 13 years, owned by my son Alex, gifted to him by my deceased brother John. It was a riddle, a piece of my puzzle, a hidden message from John to complete the picture of my dream.

John knew I was brave and strong, but he also knew I had lost faith in myself. He wanted me to find that book and remember the dream so I would see the answer as clear as I saw the blue sky within those dark branches. I could not solve my problems by going around them. I had to go through them, to feel the hardship, to struggle even, to find my strength and recapture my belief in my abilities. I needed to go forward and look up to God for strength as well. I needed to do all this alone, without the physical help of others. I also needed to remember while I stepped on my, "I can't" attitude and crushed its' negative energy, that my brother's spirit would be with me all the way. A comforting thought to have.

I took the dream, the message from John, the quote in the children's book and used them to start a new philosophy called, "If I can't find a way, I will make one!"

I will not just try to juggle it all or make a go of my business ventures, but I will accomplish exactly what I want and succeed. I will be successful for myself and my children. I will show them how strong their mom can be. While I handled their lives and all the duties of a stay-at-home mom, I would start my long awaited landscaping business. It is easy to market something you believe in. So, I marketed myself to everyone I knew. I was skilled, confident and patient. I used the old "wait" attitude and waited for opportunities to present themselves to me. I was patient, ready, and organized.

Spring roared in and so did my new life toward success. While my kids were in school, I worked hard until two each day on the yards of neighborhood friends. I took each day one at a time.

I was managing my present and it felt great. I never pulled back on my duties as a mom, but with every fiber of my being found a way to develop a business that worked for me.

I have only just begun this new venture and schedule so I am sure there will be tweaks and hiccups in my plan, but I will cross those bridges as I come to them.

I just keep repeating to myself, "I can do this!"

I AM GOING TO BE AN ANGEL TO ALL PEOPLE.

Chapter 11

My Purpose

"I am bringing to the world the fullness of the mission that is my own"
-Elizabeth Clare Prophet

I have been asking and wondering since I was a child what my purpose in life was. We all find ourselves contemplating our existence from time to time unsure if we are fulfilling our purpose here on earth. Unfortunately, the answer to this age old question... What is my purpose... cannot be researched or found on a search engine like *Google*.

It is easy to place the responsibility in God's hands and wait till we die to receive our answer, but I do not want to do that. I want and need to figure it out now, so I can grow spiritually and emotionally. It is important to me. Though I hate to hang on to "Time" it is in this portion of my life that time is of the essence. So, I begin my journey inward. It is time to look at my life in its entirety and review my thoughts and memories to see if I can find clues there. I am starting to think and feel that my purpose in life is not a solo act. Could it be possible that I have many missions to carry out while alive? I feel strongly that I do. I am a crafty juggler of many talents. I have come to see that my life is like a beautiful tree. I am strong rooted and always changing with the seasons. I am at times showing my best side beautiful in color. I am also at times bare and vulnerable. The harsh problems of my life reveal great weathering of my spirit. With each year comes regrowth and new blooms, and I get to cycle forward with hope and a fresh outlook. I adapt and dance with the happy winds of experience and knowledge. I feel the warmth of the sun which brightens my path and assists me in standing tall and proud. I have a purpose. I have many. So, you are probably wondering if I know what they are.

Yes I do! I have taken time to truly understand who I am, where I am going, and the kind of person I want to be while on my own journey. First and foremost, I am a child of God. I am a believer of all that is good and holy. I am a proud Catholic, a Good Samaritan, and an angel who will do all I can while my stay on earth is permitted. I will do right by each and every person I encounter. Without knowing where I stand in my faith, I cannot build a relationship with God, myself or others. I need to begin with the purpose of why I am a Catholic and what that means to me. It is the foundation where every other part of my life and existence is built. Thankfully, my faith in God is strong and I am committed to that. It has strengthened the floor beneath me in order to walk through the rest of my life. If I am like a tree, than it is the water that God gives me that keeps me alive and healthy. Without it, I would dry up and die. So I need Him and I need His faith to allow me to grow new branches. Each branch on my tree represents another portion of my life or experiences that I have lived through. I am maturing and will never stop growing.

Knowing my purpose as a Catholic, leads me toward all the other purposes I may have here. For example, my purpose as a friend, a sister, a daughter, a mother, and a partner is critical to examine. I do not think nor have I ever that my purpose lies in my professions or academic accomplishments. I do see the importance that those fields play in my life through the teachings and experiences they have given me. However, it is in my varying roles as a person that I find the most reward and greatest value.

My purpose here is simple. I am to be an angel to everyone I meet; to spread hope and love where it is needed. I encounter so many people each and every day. I listen to their problems, watch them struggle, feel their pain and sorrow. I know I cannot help them all. I know I cannot be with them all the time. I know I cannot dedicate all I have to each and every one. What I can do is obvious though. I can take hold of the moments and opportunities that come before me and assist in small parts of their healing. I do not have to fix everyone I know. I do not have to be their solution to a problem. What I can do is be that hand that reaches out to hug them when they need it. I can be a shoulder to cry on. I can be the person who makes them see that tomorrow is another day to handle the rest.

We all share this purpose in life to help those around us, yet some of us choose to ignore it. We become so wrapped up in our own problems that we lose sight of the struggles of others. We forget and ignore that there are problems greater than ours, and push our way through life in a boat full of complaint and regrets. I got off that ride a long time ago. I realized sailing conditions were just not right and found a different way to travel. I am glad I did. Along the way, I have met amazing people and taken the time to view breath-taking acts of kindness. My purpose is clear and rests calmly in the hands of God. I am to be the best "me" I can be.

At the end of this chapter I challenge you to take a break. Sit and think. Take a long hot shower or go for an evening stroll. Think not of yourself, but of just one person you know that could use some help. Go now and call them. Reach out to them. Be someone's angel today. You never know... you may just turn out to be the purpose in someone's life that makes all the difference.

THANK YOU
FOR
EVERY
OPPORTUNITY
TO
BECOME
A BETTER
ME!

Chapter 12

Thank You!

Dear God: Thank You for EVERYTHING!

Two words we just don't say or hear enough. Funny part is lately I have lost sight of all I am thankful for because of a small obstacle that got in the way of my recent landscape business. Only months into my career I was suddenly forced to quit work due to tremendous hand and wrist pain. A trip to the doctor proved my worst fear as a landscaper… severe nerve damage to both hands. I was instructed to stop working and schedule two surgeries immediately. My right hand carrying the worst injury was operated on first. I am typing now one handed wearing my cast. The second surgery will be a month from now. Summer vacation and the first surgery came neck and neck. Four children home and no camp complicated the overall positive outlook I have been holding for some time now. So, what else could I do but blow up some balloons and throw myself a pity party. I hate when I feel down and depressed. It only complicates my life and everyone around me.

During this time, my parents are preparing for a move

to a new home after thirty-five years. I guess it does rain when it pours! I want to help my parents with all they need to do, I need to entertain my kids all summer with play-dates, sleepovers and day trips to keep busy, and I need to figure out how to find a new career path all at the same time. Yes, all while being one handed all summer long. No time for rest or nurse my injuries back to health… just, "No time at all!"

With all this happening between the months of June and August, I need to stop feeling like everything and every situation is out to get me, and start reaching inward where my deep faith lies and find my gratitude. Instead of cursing the fact that my kids are home all summer with me, I need to embrace the memories we are creating and time we spend together. It won't be long before friends will be more important than mommy time. I am blessed to have this summer home with the kids relaxing on the beach or going to an amusement park. By next summer NOT working is just not going to be an option for this family financially.

While I have time to reflect on all I am thankful for, I also have time to reflect on new career choices. I have always known deep down inside what I should be doing with my life, but have not fully put my idea into action. It is with thanks and gratitude that my true profession is based. I mentioned within this book my life as a Psychic/Medium. I have spent years working privately doing readings for individuals and groups throughout Long Island. I am absolutely grateful for this gift of higher knowledge and spiritual connection. I do not feel embarrassed or cursed by this gift, and it wasn't until my surgery on my right hand that I realized it is what I need to pursue.

In the days that followed after my hand surgery I found myself running to the local drug store to pick up some Tylenol for my pain. While I waited on the longest line I have ever seen, my attention was directed inward. When a spirit is trying to talk to me, they either show me pictures in my mind like a scene from a movie of their life or that of the person they would like me to connect to here in the physical world. I can also hear them, feel their presence, experience different smells or sensations (not all good either, may I add). So, while I waited for the line to move it began. Here is what I heard:

"My name is James. My son is standing in front of you. Tell him it is time to throw out my motorcycle helmet."

It is very rare that I will approach someone publically. I find it can be an invasion of their privacy as well as may make them uncomfortable. I prefer to read only people who have asked me to or booked an appointment with me. However, sometimes, I will make an exception. Spirits can come to me at anytime and anywhere, but respectfully, many understand that my time is mine and I am left alone to take care of my needs for the day. Today was different though. This father's presence had something important to say I just felt it. Nervously, I tapped the large broad shouldered man on the back praying he would turn and greet me with a smile. Here is how our conversation went:

"Yes, can I help you?" the stern faced man spoke with a deep hard voice.
"No, it is me who needs to help you!" my timid voice shook nervously.

The man, of course appeared puzzled, I continued on…
"I have a gift, one I do not push upon strangers. However I have a message from your dad." I sighed with relief as the words confidently poured out of my mouth.

"What?" The man's voice softened.

"Yes, your father passed recently didn't he?" I asked the question even though I already knew the answer.

"Yes, he did." His face looked as though it hurt to focus on my words.

"Your dad is safe, not in pain. I know he was killed accidently two months ago. He tells me to tell you to throw out his motorcycle helmet. He is talking to me right now. He said today is the first day you have left your house since the accident. He is worried about you. He wants you to let him go now because he will not leave until you are ok." The words broke the silent air around us.

"How do you know all this? Are you some kind of psychic?" He spoke slowly as if in shock.

"I have a gift. Today I give it to you. You needed to hear from your dad. It is time for you to live life and celebrate your dad's life not continuously mourn it. Grieving is forever. It doesn't just go away after some time. But you can learn to laugh and be happy again. Your dad is living just in a different way. So you must now do the same." My heart broke for this man.

He did not speak to me right away, but leaned over and hugged me as we stood there in line. The woman at the register called him to move forward so he released his grip and quickly moved ahead. He completed his transaction and headed for the door. I was next on line and after bagging my items and heading outside, I saw the man standing by his car with his head in his left hand.

I walked over to him again and said, "Your father's name was James and you are not sure what to believe right now. He died on April 29, in a motorcycle accident. You put a black leather glove in his coffin. Your dad is telling me all this to validate information so you know this message today is real. Oh and he told me to tell you one more thing. Every time you guys got ready for bed the last thing he would say to you was, "'tomorrow we conquer the world bud.'" I reached my hand up to pat his back as I walked away. I got in my car and sighed deeply. So many people hurt in this world for so many reasons. I pray that man found peace in my words. He waved to me as I drove off and I smiled and waved back. At that moment I felt grateful for my gift. So many people have lost loved ones including me, and today I made a difference in someone's life.

I started to really think about the many readings I have done over ten plus years. The kind people I have met. The believers who always wanted to know beyond what their religion, or mind told them. The skeptics who questioned my beliefs and abilities yet always were pleasantly surprised by my information. I have been making a difference in all these stranger's lives for some time, but never really appreciated or gave thanks to God for giving me such a unique gift. Maybe this is what I am meant to do? Maybe this should be my career?

I am not sure what I am going to do yet but plan on giving it real thought. I know I should be able to see and predict the outcome of my own life, but that is not always so. Every day brings new clues and feelings, but I need to determine the true meaning behind them. If I do decide to make my career one of the supernatural kind, then with all the support I may receive from friends and family, I must too face the criticism from the outside world. How will this affect my children? I must always put them first and decide what is best for them. I feel I need a sign, another BIG gesture from above to help me find my way.

God has many plans for me, but is this one of them? So many questions I have and who do I turn to for guidance and help?

God, I am listening....

NOT EVERYONE IS CAPABLE OF HANDLING ALL YOU GO THROUGH.

Chapter 13

No One Understands Me!

Not every person shares the same experiences!

Are we all alike in one way or another? Of course! It is funny how many people I have met during the past few years going through a divorce or a career change. Every story is different and so unique, yet we share a common bond of pain and loneliness. What I learned most of all is who I can count on during the difficult times. It is amazing how many people run away from you as if you have the plague. I am just getting divorced, but somehow they think my situation threatens their lives. It is like having the cooties and everyone might catch it if they continue to talk to you.

No one understands what I have lived through and what I continue to go through. Some try to understand me. There are so many though who do not and never will. They are just not capable of handling all I am going through, yet they are not the ones struggling with my problems.

It is easy to run away from what seems difficult. It is easy to stay away from others who suffer so not to get dragged down with them. People are afraid of people and afraid to extend themselves to help others.

I am not disappointed or angry at those who have not been there for me through my divorce or personal changes. No one has lived my life, thought my thoughts or felt the emotional charge of my actions. No one I know can see the dead, feel or speak to them, so they cannot understand how much of who I am is based in that. I know there are many out there like me. There are many psychic/ mediums in this world, but I do not know any personally. There are many women my age with children going through a divorce, yet I do not share the same experiences with them. So this time of my life is lonely and somewhat of a solo act. I do have my support system, but I must figure out so many things on my own.

A few months back, I met a wonderful woman while on a landscaping job. We seemed to hit it off and even though she and I come from different walks of life, we seem to share feelings in common. Recently, I had the pleasure of reconnecting with her and giving her a reading. She is a kind person who not only enjoyed her session with me, but has gone out of her way to befriend me. Together, we are brainstorming on ways to further my career as a psychic/medium.

It is in this new friendship that I have come to pursue full-time the unusual career as a Psychic Medium. For me, I have always known deep down inside that this was where my life would end up, but it took the faith that another had in me to jumpstart my supernatural career publically. My friend is now my manager and together we have set out to rebuild our lives. I believe in her just as much as she believes in me, and we are two souls that were destined to unite.

Life is now truly forming and taking on a whole new shape. My children are excited about my new career and always knew themselves that this was their mommy's comfort place. I may have taken the long road to get here, but the journey was so worth it. I am still functioning as a stay at home mom and doing all I can for my children, but I am constructing a new business now one that at times will pull me away from my children. My biggest fear has finally come. How will I do it all? This is the type of career that requires evening work and weekends, but I can no longer run from that idea. I will find my place and how my entire family will fit into it. The funny part of making the choice to go public as a psychic medium is that I need to do one very important thing.

It is time for me to "Come out" to my family and community. Today starts my real journey!

STEP OUT AND SHOW EVERYONE WHAT YOU ARE MADE OF.

Chapter 14

The Coming Out

Come out... Come out... where ever you are!

I have been working as a Psychic Medium privately for over 10 years. Deciding to work as one publicly is very different though. You see, with the exception of my mother and three living brothers, no one else in my family knows about my gift. My father, my aunts and uncles, my cousins (well most) do not know this side of me. My close friends have known for years, but there are so many others who do not. I did not intentionally hide it, well, maybe I did. I just never felt the time was right or knew how to explain what I could do. It wasn't until I attended a support group for another reason that I decided to come out to my father. I knew once I did that, everything else would fall into place. My story is oddly normal.

One Sunday morning while out and about doing some errands I decided to call a friend to say hello. I asked if she wanted to go buy groceries with me. I could hear through the phone the rustling of papers. She quickly responded that she would love to come with me, but she was about to run to a support group for her son who had come out over a year ago. I quickly volunteered to attend the support group with her hoping that my presence would help add some ease to her nervous voice. She gladly accepted my offer and before I knew it I was waiting at the door of her beautiful home. We chatted nervously the entire ride to the office where the meeting was being held.

We parked the car and found our way down a long hall to the left of the lobby. Far in the belly of the building, tucked away in a corner classroom decorated for pre-school aged children, sat over twenty adults. All these people shared something in common, yet so unique and alone in their feelings and thoughts. I was impressed by the turn out and courage of these strangers who came together to help each other grow in the learning process of raising a gay child.

I sat quietly at first, looking around at the faces of people I did not know; I felt like a child with a secret myself. I realized while each person began to share their story and explain what it was like when their child came out for the first time… that I had never been honest with my father. I was still living in my own closet sort of speak, and I wanted out too.

Some parents seemed so controlled and full of acceptance, while others were fresh in the thick of their child's coming out party. Some embraced the news and some did not. It made me think. "Would my father love me or accept me for what I was? Would my mother be alright spreading the news that she has a child who can talk to the dead? If I come out publically, I do not just expose my secret… I expose my entire family to the whispers and sometimes negative comments of others. Could they all cope with that?" I sat back and listened some more.

With each story I felt my fear grow and subside like a dizzy roller coaster ride. The group broke for a short recess and idle chatter was sent throughout the room. Some people chose to comfort others in the room. Others sat still in their chairs lost in daydreams of a safe and easy life for their children. I sat feeling humbled and proud of these brave parents who showed a deep strength and love for their children, yet most of them would never tell their sons and daughters about attending this support group. How they must all love their children so much that they would all step out of their comfort zone and expose their secret lives to others.

A guest speaker attended this support group. His name is John Schwartz. You may have heard of him. He wrote a book entitled Oddly Normal. The book describes his life story and experience regarding his own son's sexuality. He is not just a great speaker, but an amazing writer, father and husband. I do not know him personally but have always followed his work as a New York Times correspondent. I was eager to hear him speak and share his knowledge with the other parents. At the end of his speech most of the parents rushed to the back of the conference room to purchase his book. I too made a purchase even though none of my children have come out. I figured this book was not just for parents with gay children. This book was an inspirational story of hope, love, and coming to terms with being different. I needed to read this story. I am different. I am hiding in my own closet and hoping to finally come out to all I know… mostly my dad.

Having my dad approve of my lifestyle is important to me. No matter how old I grow, he is still my father and I am his little girl. I want him to be proud of who I am and who I continue to become. The more my name spreads across Long Island as an established Psychic Medium, the more I would run the risk of my world and his world colliding. I needed to be upfront and honest. It was time I came out.

My friend and I left the support group changed people. I set out to attend this meeting in order to help my friend. Ironically, it was she who helped me. Maybe she was meant to take me to that location. Maybe it wasn't her who needed to learn and grow. She continues to support her son silently. So does her husband. He is a typical teenager always thinking his parents do not understand him. He is lucky though. He just needs to mature to see that. Their worry and questions define uncertainty to him, yet it is through their worry and questions that they show how much they love their son. If they did not care, did not love him, did not support him, they would have disowned him. In time, yes time, he will see how blessed he is and how thankful he should be for their kindness and love.

So, here I am... leaning against the inside of my closet door looking for the courage to turn the knob and push my way out. What waits for me on the other side I do not know, but at the age of forty-one it is time for me to find out! So it will once again be through fear and strength that I step out of my comfort zone. Thoughts racing through my head, my stomach full of nervous swirls, I need a sign from someone to let me know what I am about to do will be alright.

As I brush my teeth that night getting ready for bed, my mind cannot seem to shut down. My kids are still at their dad's house, and the silence in the air is deafening. I climb in my bed and decide to meditate on my thoughts of coming out. As my eyes grow heavy and I take one last scan around the room, I catch a glimpse of a shadowy figure to my left. Believe it or not, it is oddly normal for me to see spirits at night especially at bed time. They love to come in my room touch my things and talk to me. Usually, the dead are very awake and lively to me, so the word dead in my definition is not what you might define it to be. If I could create my own definition to the word it would go something like this: Dead: when those who are not here in the physical sense appear to us spiritually and talk and talk and talk...

So, before I can actually go to sleep, I must see who it is and try to find out what it is they need or want from me. Much of the time the spirits who visit me are people I do not know. This time, I felt a familiar presence. I focused my eyes toward the figure and the dark shadowy blob grew clear with color and shape. Standing before me was my grandpa on my mother's side of the family. (She will find out while reading this book of my recent visit from him.) He walked to the end of my bed and slowly sat down facing me. We stared at each other and without moving our lips, we spoke. Our thoughts raced in conversation and I felt tears fill my eyes longing for his love. I told him of my day and my fears about coming out to my dad and rest of the family. He sat quietly and listened. Then, when I was done he spoke echoing in my head the true sound of his voice.

Why are you afraid of who you are and what you represent for this family? You are special and different. We up here like you this way. If so many of us up here accept you, so will your parents. Your dad will understand, somehow, he will learn to understand you. Believe in him. He loves you. What he does not understand, explain to him. He will listen. He will be proud of you. You have gone through so much. We all see that up here. We believe in you. Now sleep and have faith that tomorrow will bring you answers to all your questions.

I do not remember my grandfather leaving the room or fading from view. What I do remember is waking to the darkest morning yet. The sky was not visible and the road from my window just a memory, but in my dark quiet box of a room, I felt my vision was clear and sharp. Today I would come out. Today I would see exactly what I was made of. Today my father would no longer see me as his little girl who struggled for the past three years. Today, I would show everyone, living and dead, how strong I really was. No more hiding behind closed doors. This game known as my life was about to get very real, and I was going to be the Seeker. Kids know all about playing hide and seek, and that is the game I have been playing with myself for a long time. Today was different though, today I was going to start a new game.

LOOK
WITH
YOUR
MIND
AND
HEART
NOT YOUR
EYES.

Chapter 15

I See Dead people

Will you still love me even though I am different?

One day after attending the support group for parents with gay children, I gathered up the strength to confront my dad. He was eager to sit with me after I expressed I had much to discuss with him. We sat at a small round table in the heart of my dining room and began our conversation. My father is a very gentle man, always there for his children. Yet, for some reason, I felt afraid to confront him regarding my gift as a Psychic/Medium. He has never judged any of his children and has been an incredible role model and advocate for our family. My entire life I have felt love and support from my father. During the loss of my brother and even during the struggles of my divorce, my father was always there for me. No matter what his personal pain was, he never relaxed in his role as husband and father. He is the kind of man I hope my own sons grow up to be like.

Before I could begin my confession of my secret life, my father interrupted my thoughts with a question.

"Mary, what are those bottles behind you in that corner hutch?" my dad looked confused.

I turned around to see what was behind me. "Here we go," I thought. I had some promotional items in a cabinet in the dining room for different events I was working on. The water bottles green in color had the words Mary Drew North Shore Psychic Medium on them. I sighed with relief knowing this was my segway into our first of many conversations.

"Those belong to me for my new business dad." I sat quietly waiting for his next move.

"What do those words mean?" his face, obviously puzzled.

"Dad, I work privately as a Psychic Medium. I can talk to the dead, even see them. I give people readings and have been for many years now. But recently I have gone public with it. I am starting to book large events at restaurants and continue to assist in fundraising for various causes." The words flowed with ease off my tongue and my heart cheered for my bravery.

"Oh, I see. Ok. That's good. But I do not understand what you mean exactly. Explain it to me," My dad listened wholeheartedly.

"A medium is someone who connects to people who have passed away. I can hear them, see them, feel them and even see pictures in my mind about things they show me. They tell me about their lives, their family or friend's lives, and about things that are still yet to happen. As a psychic, I can feel and know things about a person I have never met. I can tell them about their private experiences. When I schedule a session with a client I only take their first name and cell number. Unless the person gives me their last name on a voice mail message, I do not take that down during a phone call at all. This way no one can claim I Googled them or found them on some social media website." And with those words, I sat back in my chair while my soul applauded silently.

The news was out. The message was given. My dad thought

about what I said and asked to see the green water bottles behind me. I pulled one out from the cabinet to show him. He held it in his hand and gazed over at me with a smile on his face. He asked two very fatherly questions.

"Is this safe what you do? Can you support the kids financially doing this?" My father waited patiently for my answer.

"Yes dad, I have taken the proper safety precautions and formed a legitimate corporation which handles my financial assets. I even took on a Manager. I am busy dad. I am making a name for myself. I am doing what I was meant to do and love to do. I am making it as a single mom." As the words blew off my breath I could feel myself fighting not to cry.

Every word I spoke to my father was mostly true. He has been under so much stress worrying about my survival after my divorce. Though numerous people in my family offered to help me financially get on my feet, I could not accept any of their offers. I needed to hit the bottom, to struggle, to know what it was like to live paycheck to paycheck, month to month. I needed to stand on my own two feet from the start. I am proving to everyone, mostly myself, that I will not just survive this experience but live graciously through it. Divorce takes a long time and with that-being-said, can rob one of any money they had. Thankful for child support and a little maintenance, I was able to float above water through it all, but as we all know, lawyers are expensive and much of what I have gathered has paid for that.

My father rose from his chair and stepped closer to me. He hugged me and whispered in my ear.

"Can I go to one of your events?" He smirked as he looked at the reaction on my face.

"Of course you can. I want you and mommy to. Will you come?" I was excited at the possibility.

"My daughter is going to be famous and I will be there to see it happen!" he proudly stated that comment as if it were so.

My dad left shortly after that to head back to his house. I quickly ran to the phone to call my oldest brother, Mike, and tell him all about what had just happened. We talked for a while, laughing and giggling at the thought of dad and mom watching me preform. Then it hit me that even though I had already worked a few events on Long Island, none of my brothers had seen me work as a Psychic Medium. So, there on the phone, I invited my brother Mike to my next event weeks away. I told him I would be in Oakland Gardens, Queens at a restaurant called Anthony's Italian Cuisine. Mike lives in the city with his wife Mary and I thought they just might be able to take a car service over. Mike promised me he would be there. I knew in those words that the reservation would be set the next day. My brother has always supported me and never gone back on a promise. I am blessed because, all my brothers support me and have been so kind. The baby girl and only-girl for that matter, of five kids can leave one spoiled by the affections of her older siblings. I have four amazing brothers. One watches over me from heaven, while the rest watch over me from earth. I am grateful for them all.

I hung up the phone excited and refreshed. What a day I had! First, my dad's approval, and now my brothers word to see my next event. I am feeling really happy. There are just two more weeks till my next event. I better get my mental groove on and start creating only positive thoughts. No single event is more important than another. Each one is meaningful and special to me. However, this one was going to be different. This one was going to contain two special guests, Mike and Mary. They were going to be the first people in my family to ever experience my gift.

It's show time!!!

APPRECIATE ALL YOU HAVE AND THE PEOPLE IN YOUR LIFE WHO HAVE ALWAYS LOVED YOU!

Chapter 16

Table for Two

Appreciate the people that have been there for you through your ups and downs because those are the people that love you the most.

The night was approaching to the event I was scheduled to work in Queens. I was excited at the news of a sold out show, but even more excited to hear that one of the reservations made was by my brother Mike. Just as he promised, he and his lovely wife were attending this nights' event.

My favorite part about going to a large group reading is the mystery behind each person who comes. I almost never recognize a face in the crowd except for the occasional attendance of a friend supporting me. Tonight would be no different than all the others, strangers walk through the door, and new friends and clients walk out.

I enjoy connecting to the people who have passed away, but more importantly, I enjoy creating bonds with the people who desire the readings. Most people who come to a session are believers in spirit activity or an extension of life after death. However, many others will come along with friends or family members who are skeptical and not sure about what I do. Many have even prejudged or developed assumptions about me prior to attending. They imagine me sometimes gypsy-like crystal ball and all; they imagine me to be some kind of witch or mind reader.

I am none of those things… and the looks and expressions on their face when they first set eyes on me says it all. My job is simple and clear. To deliver messages from deceased loved ones. I am to hand over the information to the client, not have the client feed clues or pieces to a puzzle I am to figure out. My job is to shock and awe the group with the knowledge of their lives or their relatives' lives that I could and should not know.

The experience began around seven-thirty on a Friday night. After a long work week, people had gathered together for great food, drinks with friends, and a spiritual connection to the other side. I watched as the crowd rolled in, excited and chatty. While I wait for the event to begin, I remove myself from the room after my audio equipment has been set up. I do not like to stay in the room as people nervously speak with friends at their tables. I never want to be accused of listening in or over-hearing conversation.

My events always begin the same way. I take time to explain who I am and how the night will unfold. There are many who have never been read or attended a large function like this, so it is important to explain how it works and what they should expect. During the introduction speech, time is given to the audience to settle down, relax their nervous energy, and begin my connection to the other side.

That night, the room was full and large tables of women sculpted the room's décor. I glanced in the dining area to see if my brother and sister-in-law had arrived. Seated at a small square table covered in white linen was my first family member to attend an event of mine. My heart leaped with excitement. Tonight, I would not just wow the crowd I would change the relationship with my oldest brother forever. He was already a great supporter of mine, but now it was time to have him see my calling.

My brother Mike glanced in my direction. Normally, I am not nervous, but now butterflies were dancing inside my stomach. He gave me a wink and sweet loving smile. I suddenly began to relax. I knew at that moment no matter how the night unfolded, he would be proud of me.

Two hours and 22 minutes exactly, the event lasted. One of my longest performances in a restaurant.

I am usually meant to read the audience for an hour-and-a-half which is separate from the introduction and question period. The room was full of life and electric energy. As I wished everyone well and turned to shut down the mic and amp system, I stole a second look toward my brother's table. I never read him or my sister-in-law Mary, but I had no intention to either. Mary was wiping tears from her eyes with a table napkin. Mike was beaming ear to ear with a smile that transcends any look he has ever given me.

I was pleased with myself, and not because I impressed the audience or gave them the best readings of their lives. I was happy because my brother knew the truth about me. He was supportive and loving and without judgement. I had nothing to fear. It is funny how dead people do not scare me, yet sometimes it is the living souls that make me feel doubtful or unsure.

Michael walked away that night knowing he was going to place a call to my parents the next day. He was going to speak on my behalf and share his experiences and mine with the two people I need approval from the most. I have never truly questioned my families love and commitment to me. It is only natural though to assume that all that encompasses me may not apply to their spectrum of understanding or comfort.

I woke the next morning as I always do after an event… tired and depleted of energy. Reading people has that effect on me, especially when dealing with a large group. I decided to lay in bed using images from the night before to entertain my thoughts. I could not help but wonder what Mike and Mary must have discussed on their ride back to New York City. Did he call our parents? And if he did, what did they say? I rolled my tired body to the edge of my bed and grabbed my cell phone from the black charger that held it tight. I swiped the screen and saw I had two texts. Here we go.

Text 1 read: "Hey Weenie…it's Mikey!" (Yes, my brother calls me that!)

"Mary and I had the best time last night. You were amazing! I do not know how you can do what you do, but now that I have seen it with my own two eyes, I have no doubt in my mind that you are one special girl. I love you."

"P.S. I called mom and dad."

Oh God! Hesitant to check the next text, I managed to swipe the screen again and look. There it was… my mom sent me a text. She is rather new at texting, so I could not help but giggle at the thought of how long it may have taken her to write this message.

Text 2 read: "Rise and Shine! Guess who? It is your mother. Call me when you wake up. Not sure what your schedule is like today. Mikey called me. We can't wait to speak to you. Lol" (my mom at this time in her life thought "Lol" meant "Lots of Love")

I Smiled. I sat up in bed and prepared myself for a call that could go either way. Their house phone rang four times before my dad's voice echoed through the receiver, "Hello Drew, Mary! How is my famous daughter?" My dad sounded so bright, clear and happy. He sounded… proud!

"I am good daddy, what are you doing?" I asked but knew exactly what he would say.

"I am making your mother coffee. The Princess is still half asleep. She is eager though to talk to you so I better put her on. Hold on a minute. How are the kids? What are they doing?" My dad asked.

"Everyone here is good. You are a good hubby… can you come here and make me coffee too?" I teased with love.

"Anything for my girl! Ok, good. Tell kids Pop Pop misses them. Here is mom. Love ya baby!" I could hear my dad passing the phone over to my mom.

"Hello Madi-ooch." My mom has a thousand nicknames for me.

"Hi mom, you awake?" I questioned because her voice was

tired and shaky.

"Yes, barely. So, heard you are a rock star!" She laughed.

"Oh no, why? What did Michael say?" Wishing I was a fly on the wall to hear that conversation.

"Mikey said you were shocking. He told dad and me that we have to go to one of your events. We want to come. Soon as we get settled in, we are coming to an event ok?" She paused to answer my father in the background who was anxiously looking for some item he misplaced. "Mary, I need to go help your dad find his glasses, can I call you back?"

"Of course. Call me later. I am going to get in the shower anyway." I always feel better after the water hits my face and washes the lingering energy fragments way from the night before.

"Ok sweetie, call you later. Come by with the kids. We miss them. Oh and one other thing, I am so proud of you." My mom's voice faded in the distance as she hung up the phone.

So there it was, the word I so wanted to hear, "Proud!"

My parents always are, but this was different. I needed to hear it. I longed to be awarded with praise as a child does after reading a passage well or drawing a picture. I felt like a child again. I just want them to know that their love and support is all I ever need to get from one day to the next. Life was really expanding and changing these days. I never thought I would even share my gift with the world nor my family. Today, I feel happy. Today, I am whole.

I am going to savor this feeling for a little while longer as I pull the sheets back over my head. I feel like I could fall back asleep, something I never do.

I am overwhelmingly tired all of a sudden. I hear the kids starting to stir in their rooms. Maybe one more minute of peace before the storm fronts rush in.

Just maybe!

I WILL DANCE IN THE RAIN AND SING THROUGH THE STORMS, ALWAYS!

Chapter 17

When it Rains... It Pours!

Why is everything changing all at once?

A move, a New Career, Illness... Oh My!!!
"The part of Dorothy will be played today by Mary Drew." Yikes! How did I get tossed into so many storms and spin out of control? Just as my excitement and energy builds mentally to create a strong step forward, a huge gust of wind knocks me back.

When I was married, my husband and I purchased a charming home we referred to as the Tree House. The small three bedroom house was nestled within its' structural imperfections. I loved this house. Large backyard fenced in for my kids and dog. To me, this house and the village of Sea Cliff was perfect. Sea Cliff is a small village, about one square mile, of friendly people who all seem to know one another. It is a unique little hippy town often referenced as, "Mayberry." All I knew was... I fit in here! But with divorce comes many changes and within those legal documents a loss of more than just a relationship. Everything was about to change.

The kids and I moved in May of 2014. Keeping the ONE promise I made to my kids, we traveled only a few minutes away to another development within the arms of a town called, Glen Head.

This neighboring community to Sea Cliff is beautiful and alive with its own unique charm. Best part, it kept my kids in their school district keeping my promise. Leaving was not an option for the children because of the solid friendships they created and a sense of stability within their school family. Plus, I had just begun a business here. My parents too, had settled into a new community an hour from us, so losing the support of our district would be a great set back next to being separated from my folks. We rearranged some things and found a way to stay. Exhausted from the move, the school year, divorce, and a thousand other changes, I welcomed summer's breeze and the rest it carried in.

Every summer my children are fortunate to spend a week away with their father visiting his family. I am sure after a fast-paced move and finals behind them, they were looking forward to fun in the sun. Did I mention what I would be doing? I am getting to that. One week… no kids… equals… Work, Work and more Work. You thought I was going to say SLEEP didn't you? Not even in the cards. I planned a full week of work and organized our new house. Rentals are a great way to get on your feet for a single mom. There was and still is no way I could afford to purchase a home on the North Shore of Long Island. Prices are high and kids are expensive. Not to mention, my lawyers and accountants have probably remodeled their entire offices on what it cost to get divorced and start a business.

While preparing for the kids to go away, I noticed how tired I felt. Of course I am tired. So many years and so many experiences would bring that forth, but this seemed different. Tasks I could do before without a thought seemed difficult. I was working a lot, had just moved, and struggled with other family issues, but something seemed odd. I have battled some health issues over the years, so it is possible my body is worn mentally and physically. In fact, my body is worn spiritually and emotionally as well. Maybe a nap is in order or even better… maybe a massage!

First thing I did after sending the kids off to Florida, was head straight for the nail salon. A little "ME" time was in order and I couldn't wait. I grabbed an ice coffee on the way in, and sat in the first open chair. After a relaxing mani/pedi, I decided to end the session with a twenty minute back massage. This was just what I needed. I climbed into the sculpted black chair and placed my face in the donut hole head rest. This was going to be just what the doctor ordered.

OOOUUUCCCHHH!

This was the longest twenty minutes of my life! Absolute torture. Every rub, squeeze and pat was like knives under my skin. I absolutely love to get a massage or my back scratched, but what the hell was this lady doing to me! I felt like I was in a boxing ring waiting for the bell to sound off. Was it over yet?

I paid and got out of there as quick as I could. I drove home annoyed at the experience. When I walked in the house, I realized once again I felt tired and achy and headed off to bed. I NEVER nap! I have to be dead to sleep. Most of the time I am an insomniac, so it was strange to feel so weak. I decided a few days later that I would go to the doctor for some routine tests.

Months later, after seeing a trillion doctors and drained of tubes of blood, I was diagnosed with Fibromyalgia, Allodynia and G.E.R.D. Fibromyalgia is a condition that many people suffer from quietly. Many of the symptoms can not be seen with the eye. A condition where nerves in the body tend to misfire and are overactive, causing severe pain, fatigue and anxiety. Allodynia tends to go hand in hand with most Fibromyalgia patients. We can experience skin irritations, numbness, burning and tingling and migraines. My G.E.R.D. (gastrointestinal issue) can cause a long list of symptoms ranging from stomach and dietary changes to chronic dry cough with throat irritations. The combination of illnesses has too many symptoms to list and takes a real disciplined lifestyle change to manage.

So, here I am. Now age 42. I Speak to the dead, am divorced, have anxiety, and now I have these wonderful disorders. I never want to be defined by my illnesses. Illness is usually a weakness of the body or mind. I prefer to label all my conditions, disorders. Why you ask? Well, it is simple. My diagnoses or all my health problems feel like a disruption of my daily functioning. My body or mind is in a state of confusion and mess, so it is natural for conditions to build or awaken from their dormant state.

I am living with anxiety, a reflux disorder, fibromyalgia and so much more… but I am not dying from them and I am definitely not a victim of them either! I am by nature a fighter, so these labels bring forth more reason to fight hard… and I will! These conditions are very real and very serious, and most days, very debilitating. I will categorize them into my file cabinet labeled Mary Drew. Depending on the day, depends on what folders are being pulled out and looked through. I have no time and no room for sickness. I have four kids to take care of. What seems to suffer the most is my business and my clients, but I am working on correcting that.

Most people, including members of my own family and network of friends, do not realize I have any of these setbacks. Most days are a struggle and a fight to get through. My disorders are hidden and silent from the outside world. Fellow parents at school pick up, a woman standing next to me in a grocery store, conversations over the phone with friends and family, and even relaxing time off with my boyfriend John is masked in physical pain and chronic fatigue.

I know when and for who, to put on a happy face and just suck it up. I know what you are all thinking. I shouldn't have to. People who love you will understand you are not well or tired. That may be true. But in the end, I am forever trying to ease others pain by hiding my own. There is no time to throw another pity party for myself and I definitely do not want any surprise parties thrown in honor of me by the ones I love. I always say, "I will either find a way, or make one." It is that small phrase that gets me through most everything I do. So, I am tired. Then I will learn to slow down. So, I am in constant pain. Then I will change my diet and exercise. If I need help, I will learn to ask. If I need sleep, I will learn to do that too (as long as my deceased friends stop keeping me up).

I am learning through hardship and set-backs that the path ahead lies in the one I pave for myself. So, if hard stone doesn't work for me anymore or obstacles become too heavy to lift and toss, I will lay before me pillows and feathers to tip toe upon.

Whatever it takes I will repaint this picture of my life to express the beauty that is within me. I do not have cancer, yet so many dear to me do. I still can recall, think, and recite the memories that are shaping my life. So many these days lose that gift. So, I am thankful and grateful for the disorders I carry and the people they connect me to. I am no different than anyone who reads this. I am struggling and in pain. But that is just one small (ok large) part of me. I am also happy and full of life. Shouldn't I focus on that instead?

I am a year and a half exactly living in my cozy rental and living with my not so cozy disorders. Strangely, I am happy with the hand I have been dealt. When my life stops twisting and we land safely on the ground, I will pray I find no striped stockings and ruby red shoes beneath me. I do not want to harm anyone when I land or during my turbulent fall. I am in need of a good witch who can wave some magic upon me.

"Oh wait, some would say, I am that witch." Maybe I better get moving and follow the yellow brick road that leads to my rainbow. I got a funny feeling that this path may have a lot more twists and turns, but I think that is ok, as long as it brings me back home.

LIFE

IS A

BALANCING ACT

THAT TAKES

PRACTICE

AND

DETERMINATION.

Chapter 18

Work –vs– Kids

"Life isn't about waiting for the storm to pass... but about learning to dance in the rain."
                                        -unknown

Dancing with the stars here I come! I wonder how much practice it takes to become a great balancing act or a dancer of a thousand dances. I think maybe I will take my act on the road and see what kind of audience I draw.

Work-life and mommy-life are two different things in most people's lives. In my life, they are polar opposites. I care for the living (my children) and I care for the dead (everyone else's loved ones). It is a very hard balancing act and keeping the see saw in a continuous horizontal position is impossible. There are so many ups and downs about being a Medium and being a Mom.

Someone I met once called me, "The Mother of all Mediums." I laughed at the thought of how I could twist this phrase around and make it my own. I am definitely a mother, but not the care-taker of all. However, as a Medium I have an obligation to the client. I am not just hired to read them. I hope to offer solutions for their grieving souls and transfer messages from beyond that help hearts to heal. After much thought, I realized I do treat my clients as if they were my children. I want them happy, safe and strong to face the outside world. I want that for everyone I encounter. I worry about my kids when they leave the house for school or for an activity. I also worry about my clients' when they leave my house full of new information to ponder.

Readings and understanding death is my life's work. So is raising four children. How can I be sure that everyone's needs are met? Well, frankly I can't. There are no guarantees that I will please everyone, raise perfect children, save every broken soul that walks through my door, or heal the world that I call my own. In order to please one or save one, sometimes others must wait. In order to handle all I do, sometimes schedules suffer and are rearranged. Many understand that life is crazy and things change from minute to minute, but along my journey in seek of balance, I have upset people unintentionally.

I have missed a few school events due to work. I have left kids home without sitters on occasion though my oldest is sixteen. I have cancelled playdates and missed family outings in order to serve clients. Most of all, I have given up most weekends to dedicate to work.

Then, there is the other side of the see saw. The seat where my clients hold tight. Too many times I have let that seat slam down and hit the ground while my children ride the opposing seat up! There have been cancellations and calendar adjustments. There have been clients pushed around so many times that rescheduling was not even an option anymore. I have disappointed others in order to handle my children and my personal life. That is not only unprofessional but it is not the kind of person I am. Unfortunately, I am a solo act. I juggle much of my life by myself. I want to take this time to apologize to anyone out there who I made wait, rescheduled, or never got to. I am not only sorry, but I am saddened by the missed opportunities to get to know some of you. I want to apologize to my boyfriend for the little time he gets with me, my friends who never see me, and myself because I find little time to take care of that aging face in the mirror.

The really upsetting part in work life and home life is that, no matter how much I love what I do, I cannot and will not ever let my kid's seat hit the ground. I love my clients. But my kids are my priority, my life, and my reason for living. I would give everything up for them and sacrifice my career and all it brings in order to be there for them when they are sad, sick, or struggling.

I am not in this profession or life for the money it provides or the fame that may or may not come along with it. I am here to serve. Sometimes I am serving my clients and much of the time I am serving my kids.

Now, I know what you are all thinking... What about the money! I provide a service and with that I get paid. What many do not see is the time I spend emailing, texting clients or taking long phone conversations for free. What many may not see is the endless amounts of money I raise for charities and organizations. It has never been my thing to expose my secrets and things I do for others that where done not for recognition but from the heart. There isn't one day that passes that I do not make a donation in some form or another.

Life is hard. Supporting kids a challenge. In knowing that, the playground time has become a permanent part of each day. I am always trying to balance it all and understand what needs must be met first. I would do this career with or without disorders, I try to work with the best of my abilities and intentions, and I do this because I know how important it is to share my gift.

I do not take anything for granted and know that it is because of my clients that my kids and I have stayed afloat. I am grateful and feel so deeply for everyone I meet. I know I am blessed with clients who support me, encourage me, and wait for me.

Along the way, I have also met some very mean people. I

think about a time when I had a death in my own family just days after my son was rushed to the doctor with 104 fever – strep again! I had to move a client who I so kindly offered to read for free. She was nasty and rude and made me feel horrible. Worst part of the story was she too is a single mom. She should know how hard it is to keep all the balls in the air, but she was cold and unforgiving. At first I felt terrible for cancelling on her. As the day went on, my guilt turned to anger and my anger turned to an unsympathetic nature. I do what I can, when I can. And no more. I am not a world famous Medium! I do not have family nearby or babysitters or a husband. I cannot afford a nanny or any type of daycare. I am not in the position of other Mediums you see on T.V. who have grown kids or spouses to fall back on.

"I need a wife!"

I love using that phrase because it is so true. There are so many successful married men who do amazing jobs providing for their families. However, it is what lies within the blurred background of a picture that tells the true story. There is usually a wife… an overworked, unappreciated, exhausted woman. Some of these wives have children and some do not. It really doesn't matter because it is the wife's job to provide an environment so sound and solid that her husband can get around gracefully.

Not all men take woman for granted. Not all woman are good wives. Not all couples function like a partnership. I never will generalize that what I may know or have experienced is what most others have. I can only tell my story. My version is long and hard and may take a lifetime to process. But I never give up and never stop trying. Having a supporting "wife" figure would be nice though. Women find so much of their happiness and value in their families/husbands successes. Women think with different goals and dreams in mind. Women strive to heal the lives that matter to them. I am one of those women. I was when I was married and still am through a divorce. I believe in building people up and making small impacts where ever I go.

Work needs to have that kind of woman run her company. Children need that kind of woman to get them through their growing years. I need that woman to be me in order to become the best Mary. I am trying. I am learning each and every day.

Today I saw the fifth grade class at Sea Cliff Elementary school put on their very own circus performance. There were jugglers, plate spinners, balancing acts and stilt walkers blind folded walking over obstacles in their path.

I giggled at the thought that this small theatrical performance was the metaphor of my life.

I just hope my show is as cute and entertaining as the students I watched. I could learn a thing or two from these kids.

Let the fear go and just have some fun.

FEEL
THE
FEAR
WITHIN
AND THEN
DO
IT
ANYWAY.

Chapter 19

Superman

Courage Is Not Living Without Fear, Courage Is Being Scared To Death and Doing The Right Thing Anyway!

Words for everyone to live by! Every time I read this quote, I think of Superman. When I think of Superman, my mind takes laps around the years of my life with my brother John. He is my superman. All my brothers are. They are heroes to me in different ways and at different times of my life.

Sitting at a desk writing helps me focus my normally crazy mind. I can't help but daydream about my brother John. He is Fifteen years gone, but it still feels like only yesterday. We use to sit together on Friday nights in Baskin Robins eating mint chip waffle cones while deciding what movies to rent. I miss talking to him. I miss seeing him. Yes, I know what you are all thinking! Aren't you a Medium? Don't you see dead people... even members of your own family? Yes, I am and yes I can, but my brother cannot and will not come to me all the time. He does leave me a great deal of symbols to find though.

Superman happens to be one of them. Every time I see someone wearing a superman shirt or come across a superman sticker, I can't help but think of John and his strength during his cancer years. I wonder if I could be as strong as him if faced with the Big C! I pray I never know, but I do see why my brother loved the comic book character.

Superman is strong, fast, can fly, and has x-ray vision. I may not be able to fly or melt metal, but my words and knowledge can help people soar past their grief. My ability to see into other people's lives and see the dead, may melt away the pain that so many harbor about death. I am definitely not faster than a speeding bullet, but my ever spinning brain can find those that shape heavens light and deliver beckons of hope and love. My strength, may not be physical, but there is a strong connection that my soul has to those living and dead. I can be strong for others when they feel weak. I am not sure how and why I have this gift, I just know that it is my responsibility to use this power carefully, honestly, and lovingly.

From the moment I saw my deceased Grandmother at the age of ten, I knew I was destined for greatness. I bottled it up for a very long time. I, like Superman, spent years hurdling toward an unfamiliar world. My journey was and still is, a long one. Once I landed safely away from my own fears, reservations and doubts, I began to grow and develop my abilities. I found a place to exist amongst the living and the dead, and life took shape in a beautiful and chaotic way. Superman found a place on earth away from the world he was born into. He made his home among the normal and the ordinary. He did all he could be like the other people around him. Then, one day, he felt the most afraid he has ever felt and began his quiet journey saving the world.

I understand how many people out there need to be saved in some-way- or-another. I have needed that myself from time to time. I realize I may be trying to save my clients, my children, and even myself by looking past what seems scary and unnatural. I have had many years to get to know me, like me, and become use to all that my brain and senses take on.

I like… No love… the idea of saving myself and the people I so deeply care about. I am my own hero these days. I defy so many laws of science and nature and I am not even sure why or how. I have a gift, one that needs to be shared and honored. We all have special talents and gifts. Some people are amazing teachers, scientists, doctors, therapists, and healers. Some people use book smarts and skills taught to them to enhance their lives or others. I am using my natural skills, learned over time through the words and pictures that my deceased colleagues provide me with. I use and choose this profession as the cape I need in order to fly. Helping others has taken me higher spiritually and mentally… Higher than I ever thought I would go.

I can touch lives all around the world with this skill or gift. That truly is a beautiful concept to embrace. My brother would be proud of me. He was a true giver and his strength and kindness his greatest power. I try each and every day to fill his mighty red rubber boots. My fears that continuously creep into my life have been the kryptonite that has held me down for so long. I may be my own hero these days, but that status comes with a cloud of doubts and fears that I may or could fail at some point or another.

My brother John never lived in fear or doubt, even when he was at life's end. If John was afraid of living or dying, he never led on to that. If John had doubts about who he was, or where he was going, he never showed me that side. He was a man of another planet and world… a magnificent creation of God.

In the Thirty-three years I got to know and love him, I really saw his greatness. No wonder God was so eager to get this angel back. He was a light not just for me to possess, he is universal. John represents to all you readers the souls you miss and mourn. Everyone reading this has lost their version of "John." In our pain and suffering, we can work hard to fly and develop our strength. In honor of so many lives lost, we should perfect our own life and live it better than ever. We need as individuals and a society to form our own version of a Justice League and fight back against the dark times.

This world is in need of Superheroes more than ever before. Ten minutes of reflecting upon our own life's problems, not to mention the entire world's issues, can really open one's eyes to how many have given up and stopped fighting their emotional and mental villains. When life gets too hard, I think of my brother John (My Superman) and remember the symbol "S."

Why you ask?

Well… if you are a nerd like me, you will know that Superman comes from the planet Kyrpton. The people born there are known as Kyroptonians. The symbol "S" in their society stands for HOPE! Something we can never lose sight of or live without.

ALWAYS LIVE LIFE WITH AN OPEN MIND AND SYMPATHETIC HEART.

Chapter 20

What am I thinking?

Mediums are not Mind-Readers or Mentalists.

A medium may have psychic abilities but not all psychics have the gift of mediumship. Anytime someone learns that I am a Medium or have Psychic Abilities, they always joke about whether or not I can read their mind. I would be a rich woman if I had a penny for every person who has said to me, "What am I thinking right now?" How the heck am I going to know that! I am not a mind reader or a mentalist.

A Psychic Medium communicates with the dead while retrieving personal information about the deceased or living person being read. The information is given to me by your deceased loved ones or my spiritual guides. We all have spiritual guides and most of us have lost someone close to us. I just happen to tune into their energy and connect. It is hard to explain to anyone who has never experienced what I have. I feel as if the electrical currents that run through my mind are linked to wires that no one can see with their human eye. My wires transmit a frequency upward or inward.

Many Mediums try to explain what they can do. Many have been tested by organizations and scientists. Every medium has their own way of receiving energy. I have heard that my gift has been compared to the way a phone call transfers from one house to another. I can see why scientists or psychics may reference that. I think there are many ways we can compare two things as having similarities. We can try with the best of our English language to explain what it is I am feeling, seeing, and hearing. This is not an easy topic and the debates will go on forever. They already have been for hundreds of years.

I am not here though to give you a history lesson about the many people who have claimed to have the gift. I am not here to sway your opinions of this topic and make you all a believer. I am here to simply tell my story to the best of my knowledge and explain why I am the way I am. Truthfully, I spend countless hours and nights lying awake in bed trying to understand why I am built this way. I will not deny that even I find it hard to believe at times that this is happening to me. I always want to think through life in a rational way and explain circumstances based on fact and science. However, this I cannot. I wish someone would explain it to me most of the time, and it is I who have to help others understand.

Spirits do not take over my body during communication nor do they change the sound of my voice. I have always believed so strongly in my faith, God, and Angels that I feel very well protected going into a reading or when spirits are contacting me. Ninety-eight percent of the time I am surrounded by good energy and positive spirits. Of course, the other two percent may be somewhat negative or a bit frightening. I have never been intentionally harmed by any spirits and believe my angelic guides protect me.

People wonder if I say protective prayers before I leave the house or when I go to bed. Actually, I do. It cannot hurt to be careful. I sure wouldn't drive a car without a seat belt to protect my body from harm. So, praying is my way of safe-guarding my soul. I frequently sage my home, myself, and even my kids rooms in order to ward off negative energy. I like my home full of laughter and goodness. There is no room for negative energy here. Living people do more than enough damage when it comes to harboring negative energy. I definitely need to protect this home and my family.

Most of the time I find that communicating with the dead is enjoyable and makes me feel good. I may feel tired after readings or after large events, but it is usually the living people who take the most out of me. The deceased are of different mindsets after a cross over. They are pure and healed of all negative traits. They mostly embody true love and understanding. Their knowledge and wisdom is far beyond what I can describe and comprehend.

The clients are the ones with setbacks and feel broken or misunderstood. It is my job to heal the living, not the dead. It is my job to pass on messages that will allow someone to view their life and experiences with a fresh outlook. When people die, they are born again into their truest form. I need to help the living transform without going through the process of death. People need to be taught how to live again or live life better. Their loved ones communicate with me in hope that something they say or a message delivered will bring about positive change and spiritual growth.

I am just the middle man... the mediator... between this world and theirs. I attempt to tune-in and am careful to try to grab hold of everything I am hearing and seeing all at the same time. There is a great deal of information being given to me all at once. Sometime I am speaking with only one spirit. And other times, I may hear the voices of many.

I do not always see who I am hearing either, that depends on the spirit who is talking to me. Some like to show themselves and others do not. I cannot explain why some shout, some are soft spoken, why some appear and others are heard, why some touch me and others only show me images in my mind's eye. I cannot explain why some family members come in during a reading and others do not. I just know that, whoever needs to talk, is who I hear.

Spirits have many places they can go and many people to visit, so it is possible that they are just not available at the time of a reading. I never promise a client I will connect with a specific person nor do I allow clients to make direct requests. It is always important to allow the spirits to decide what needs to be addressed in a reading. They have messages to deliver and the client needs to be ready to hear and receive whatever it is that may be discussed. I cannot filter a reading or pick and choose what topics should be heard. It is not up to me (the Medium) nor is it up to the listener (the client).

Mediums have become a popular topic in today's society. There are plenty of us out there and paranormal activity is researched and explored constantly. Are their fakes out there; people who intentionally set out to hurt others, lie and deceive? Of course there are. Like in any profession, there are good hearted people and bad. I can only imagine what may lie out there in the world masked as Psychics and Mediums.

There are people who are con-artists and draw pleasure and greed from other peoples' misfortunes and grief. We live in a world full of hatred, judgement and stereotyping. We live in a world where values and morals have nearly disappeared or vanished from society. Worst part about being a Psychic Medium, is I am always going to be judged and scrutinized just because of the title of my profession. I need to prove myself over and over again with every new encounter I have, every client I see, and every event I host.

Even when a good reputation follows you and recommendations give way to rave reviews, there are always doubts and skepticism tucked inside every heart. I do not mind proving my worth or working hard for what I do. I do not mind that people question my ability. That is expected and natural. What I do mind most of all, is when people publicly bully or assault others who are different. If you question or doubt something or someone, than take the time to research and gather information regarding that topic before throwing the stone kept in your back pocket.

I have thankfully only been verbally assaulted a handful of times. And when challenged, my remarks and comments are always the same. I usually tell my challenger how thankful I am for their opinions and words and then invite them to one of my shows. "Come see what I do!" I say.

Most people cannot wrap their heads around what is foreign to them or what they do not see. I get that. It is hard to really make sense out of what I do and who I am. No one has to live with me, but me. So if anyone needs to learn to accept what I am, it is myself. And fortunately, I have had Forty-plus years to learn to like and love who I am becoming. I am blessed and sure of what I am and what I can do. I am so sure of my abilities that I invite people to record sessions with me.

Mediums and Psychics are a dime a dozen these days. I advise you all to do your homework and research who it is that you chose to see. I was once told by a client that she use to see a medium once a month for over a year. I could not help myself and asked why. She said she had needed the guidance and felt that after a year this medium did not help her get closure or understanding about the loss of her daughter. I sat back and shook my head at the thought of what kind of money this woman must have spent. I asked her why she chose a Medium to see each month and not a licensed therapist. She was funny with her response. Insisting she was not crazy, she felt seeing a Psychologist or Therapist of some sort was not the way to go. So, I asked a basic question.

"Did the Medium make you feel better at all?" I predicted the answer before she could even reply.

"No. Not really." My client paused.

"A true Medium would have told you at some point within your first reading or after it was complete, that grief last forever, and the healing you were seeking will not come just because you may or may not have connected with your daughter." I sighed.

"I don't understand?" my client started to cry.

I held her hand and gave her a moment. She reached for a tissue in the floral box sitting on the table.

"People seek out Mediums to connect to people they have lost. To hear a message. I understand that and so do you. But, after that first reading or experience, the Medium should have advised you to seek out a specialist to deal with your grief and how to cope with your loss. You do not need a Medium, nor do you need to continuously pay for one, you need a friend."

"You know you will grow poor if you tell all your customers this!" my client smirked.

We both started to laugh. She is probably right. However, as much as I need money… money isn't everything. In my book of life, money will never replace honesty and common decency. I am bothered all the time at what people will do to others to benefit themselves publically or financially. I do not operate that way. Never have and never will. Later that night, after my client had left and the kids were fast asleep, I sat on my old stain covered couch and released my mind into the deepest thoughts I could. I gazed around the house scanning the mess that needed to be cleaned up and examining all that I possessed. I may not have what others have. My house may be decorated with hand-me-downs and curb side finds, my home may lack space and items we need, yet… here I am! Roof over my head and food on the table. We are rich in strength and love and hope. We are a family that fights hard each day to make it because life is so worth the effort. We are breathing… so we are okay.

I cannot help but think that we as human beings have so much to learn and so much to be thankful for. If you really want to know what I am thinking… than do not ask me if I can read your mind. Instead, ask me to help you understand life from a different perspective. Ask me as many questions as you like and I will do my best to answer them all. If I do not have the answer, than we will find the answer together. Asking questions is healthy and shows progress. It teaches us all that we seek to find solutions to things we do not understand. Mediums should always give you the information first during a reading. Anything they see or hear will be discussed. Then, when the reading is over, feel free to ask away. I am sure your mind will race with topics and thoughts that need clarifying. That is very normal and always anticipated after messages have been sent from the other side.

I may not read minds, but I can read feelings and emotions.

I feel with my heart the pain that others carry. I am assisted each and every day by my psychic abilities and the voices of the dead. It is a good thing. Keeps me on my toes and extremely alert most of the time. A medium looks like me and every other average person you pass in a store. We may not stand out or have flashing signs strapped to our chest that read, "I see dead people!"

Mediums are all around you. Some public; some private. This medium is just getting started so get ready for the new girl in town.

ALTER YOUR PERSPECTIVE ON A PROBLEM IN ORDER TO HEAL AND GROW.

Chapter 21

It's all about Perspective

A shift in your perspective may change an entire picture.

Backing out of a client's home presented some real challenges for my extremely large truck squeezed between two stone walls lining the driveway. My head bobbed back and forth examining the distance between both sides of the car. After a slow progression out onto a busy four lane street, I placed the truck in drive and took off like a bat out of hell. I was eager to leave the place I had just spent the last two hours of my life. The heaviness and negativity that created the oxygen inside Debbie's home was beginning to smother me. For privacy I have changed the name of my client in this chapter. I will refer to her as Debbie. Why you ask did I pick Debbie? Well, all I could think of as I drove clear out of sight that morning was this woman is a Debbie Downer! It is rare that I will feel this way about a client. Everyone has suffered or lost something or someone important to them. By the time they reach out for a reading, they are usually ready to hear any and all messages brought forth. I am comfortable with discussing heavy topics and helping people with grief and loss. However, Debbie was different.

Debbie had lost many people close to her which made her grief very deep and very real. She had mastered her acceptance over many years for the family members she had lost to cancer and A.L.S. She was resilient and strong in her belief that God carries the souls of all her deceased relatives. I couldn't help but feel pleased with the first twenty minutes of the reading and hearing from her departed family. But the air quickly changed and took a turn for the worst when I began to discuss her current divorce.

The struggle was long and hard and wrapped in bitterness. I did all I could to discuss with Debbie what I saw happening and how things were going to improve as long as she let go of her anger and hatred for her soon to be ex-husband. Debbie refused to see her situation for anything less than a disaster and convinced herself that the rest of her life would be full of heart ache, solitude, and misery.

She was growing physically weak from her ordeal and financially drained. Life was dark. My heart broke for her. I know first-hand how hard divorce is. So, after the reading was over, I chose to stay an extra hour with her to help her see a different perspective on life. No money exchanged. An agreement between two female hearts. I worked continuously for that hour trying to add a glimmer of hope to her future. Every word I spoke was challenged and met with distain. Debbie insisted that there was no good in this bad, and refused to hear anything I said.

My throat muscles became strained from pleading with her to see a more positive picture, but my words grew tired and began to fade in pitch. I was not going to win this argument. She had made up her mind and decided in a moment's choice, that she would live out the rest of her time in sadness, anger and a hatred so deep it was frightening.

As I drove away and turned onto the highway, my body felt weak and tired. I felt full from Debbie's anger and wanted to vomit to release the intestinal discomfort. I needed a distraction, so I turned my favorite cd on from a local group called The Brady Brothers. Their album called "Riding Shotgun" always seemed to calm me down. I relaxed the grip I had on the steering wheel, focused on the road, and enjoyed the sound of my favorite song "You Matter."

Within a few minutes I could feel my nerves release and my mind start to clear. I tried everything to stay focused on the words of the song, but my thoughts kept dragging me back to the things Debbie spoke about. There was one phrase that she said to me which really sat deep in my heart. She said, "There is only darkness now and no beauty left to see!"

Those words are foreign to me. Even in the worst times of my life, I have managed to see beauty and light. What had happened to Debbie's faith and good heart? Why couldn't she use her coping skills about death to deal with her divorce? I am beyond sick over this client and I need to find a way to get through to her. I cannot leave her heart in such a dark place.

I was half way home when I decided to turn the car around. I did not know what I would say or how I would say it, but I needed to go back to Debbie's layer of darkness and break a window or two to let in the light. The entire ride back I prayed. I prayed for someone up there to give me a sign or send me the right words to say. I needed to create a new perspective in her picture of life. But how? As I headed East on the Long Island Expressway, I noticed something I had seen a thousand times before. The sky was overcast and extremely dark. The numerous shades of gray were very depressing and rain was close by. I caught a glimpse of a section of the sky where the clouds had parted and rays of sun light streamed down to the right side of the road. The rays were golden yellow and white, thick parallel lines that touch down to the speckled brown and green grass below. The light seemed to hold my stare and put me in a trance. The entire ride back to Debbie's house I frequently glanced at the light to see if it was still there… and it was.

Then it hit me! I knew what I was going to say to Debbie. I pulled back into her driveway snug as a bug in a rug. I slid out of my door squeezing through the small crack between the wall and myself. I hurried to the door hoping she was still home. Two rings and a knock later, Debbie answered the door with a very surprised look on her face.

"Are you ok? Did you forget something?" Debbie seemed out of breath as she spoke.

"Yes, I am fine and no I forgot nothing. I need to show you something. Put on your jacket and come outside to your front lawn." I smiled nervously.

"Oh my God, is everything ok? You are worrying me." Debbie spoke quickly.

"All is fine, nothing to worry about. I need you to take a walk with me. I need to show you something." I hoped the view would wait for us.

"Ok, one second." Debbie returned with record speed and together we walked down the road. When we made a left onto the next street our view was wide and clear. I made Debbie stop and look up at the sky.

"What do you see?" I hoped for the answer in my own head.

"I see the sky." Debbie giggled.

"Good. What color is it?" I baited my hook.

"Dark grayish blue?" She questioned me as if doubted by her own vision.

"Yes! What else do you see?" I prayed now for what came next.

"Well, I see mostly clouds but I can see a section where the clouds are breaking apart and the sun is trying to peek through. There are a bunch of rays over there pulling down from the clouds." Debbie pointed with her arm in the direction of the rays.

"Right! Now look only at the rays and the part where the sun is trying so hard to be seen. Describe the sky now." I held my breath with anticipation.

"Okay. Umm, well, the rays are yellow. They are long and

kind of blurry. The specs of light seem to be hazy yet pretty. I like how they touch the tops of the trees and seem to disappear into them. I don't know. It is pretty." Debbie looked at me like I was absolutely crazy.

"Is there anything else you can tell me at this time about the rays or the sky?" I probed.

"Nope. That's all I see. Nothing else seems noticeable." Debbie looked more confused than ever.

"I guess you didn't notice that as you focused on the rays and described them to me, that the clouds around them seemed to be getting dark and heavy as if we are about to get poured on." I waited for her light-bulb to turn on but it didn't.

"I don't get it? I mean, yeah I see the sky looks ominous and dark, but the rays are what you told me to look at and describe." Debbie sighed with true frustration.

"Exactly. The entire time you focused your attention on the beautiful part of the sky you seemed to have forgotten about the darkness around you. The sky is changing and the weather is shifting toward a downward cycle, but for a moment all you saw was light and the sun trying to peek its way through. You stayed focused on the good part of the sky and not the bad. You said everything I wanted you to. In the moment, there was not only darkness but there was beauty and light. The opposite of what you said earlier." I rested my case.

Debbie looked at me and hugged me right there on the corner street as cars raced past us feverishly. I held on to her just as tight as if I had time traveled back to visit my weaker self and hug that lady too. A broken soul trying to mend itself. The client was the reflection of me from not so long ago. She was put out, tired and hurt. But she was not someone who was hopeless and doomed to live a life within the dark. I needed to save her perspective because it took a long time for me to recapture mine. Debbie and I walked back to her house and said our goodbyes. I call her from time-to-time to check on her and am happy to say she is rebuilding her new life with many windows void of curtains. No more shutting the light out or the world. She is ready to be happy, to make a choice to find her happiness, and view life in a beautiful way.

I drove home from her house for the second time. The rain pounded the roof of my car. I did not turn the music on this time or feel anxious. Instead, I drove home with my own thoughts peaceful and content.

I thought a lot about how ones perspective can make or break a situation in their life. I know it is not easy to always look on the bright side of things, to see the glass as half full, or to capture the good in the bad every time life gets hard. I, myself, have many dark dreary days when my mind takes me back to an uncomfortable time. However, as life grows on so does my perspective. I make a conscious choice to take a problem and look at it from all angles. Sometimes my view is changed rather quickly, and other times I struggle to make sense of the picture in front of me. I only know from trial and error and years of experience, that my perspective on a problem does not erase it from existence, it just makes it tolerable and full of important lessons to be learned.

Debbie reached out to me recently to schedule another reading. She happen to catch me on a bad day. Juggling family issues that seem to be splitting me in two, I was absolutely not myself on the phone. My tone was dry and weak. I felt as if the life had been sucked out of me. Debbie was very kind to notice the tone in my voice and inquired if there was anything wrong or anything she could do for me. Grateful for our conversation to snap me out of my funk, I informed her I was just trying to make some sense of a very difficult problem in my life. Debbie seemed concerned but didn't want to pry. She cleared her throat and said,

"Mary, go outside and look up. Tell me what you see." Debbie giggled.

Lazy in movement, I glanced out the window and said, "A sunny day!"

"Are you outside or inside?" Debbie probed.

"Ok you caught me. Inside. I'm going, I'm going. Hang on a second. I am grabbing my jacket it is so cold today." I shuttered at the thought of the cool air's embrace. "Alright... I am standing outside on my front step."

"Good. Now, tell me what do you see?" Debbie's voice was so perky and cute.

"Ok, I will bite. I see a clear blue sky, no clouds, no rays, it is just a solid blue." I was curious what she was cooking up this time instead of me.

"That's right. The sky is one solid mass. No variations. Just a clean blue slate. So, maybe your problem can be rebuilt from this solid place. There is nothing in your way on your journey to find the answers you need. No obstacles, no clouds, nothing. Just a peaceful blue sky."

Debbie was now the teacher and I became the student.

"Yes, Yoda. I understand what you want me to do." I laughed at her game.

"Did I Jedi mind trick you or what?" Debbie laughed so hard she snorted.

"You are right Debbie. I know that today is bright and full of ideas. I will come out of this funk happier and better because of you. Sometimes even I, forget to look up." I chuckled.

We made our appointment and got off the phone. I paced back and forth eventually making my way to the coffee machine. As I brewed a hazelnut vanilla blend I repeatedly snickered to myself that Debbie had grown so much. I guess I had grown too, but the human part of me seems to fumble along the way while the soul part of me steals the ball for a winning touchdown. Thankfully, my soul wins each and every time. Its' view is clear and extremely focused on making its' way down the field to score some points. Thank God for giving these constant reminders and the people who cross my path in order to help me to stay on task! God must have an amazing perspective from up there. He must look down and wonder how we all travel with tunnel vision most of the time. I wonder what His perspective of us and life must be. Maybe that is why He finds ways to surprise us with beautiful landscapes and skylines. Maybe His plan or wish for us is not just about love or spiritual growth. I think maybe He hopes that we can change our perspective as quick and swiftly as the weather changes its direction.

I feel like it is truly my job and my responsibility to take a client through a reading with a new and healthy perspective on life and death. It is not always going to be easy but my hard work and dedication will reward my heart and ground my thoughts. If we lose our will or desire to develop and shape our perspective on a situation, we allow our darkest feelings to creep in and weather our soul. No one wants a cold cloudy soul. We all dream and want those sun rays reaching down from the clouds shedding light on our problems. Some days the light is given to us through faith, our friends or our family members love and support. Sometimes the light is barely visible, but its warmth can be felt around us. There isn't a day that goes by that I do not reach for the light. It has become my life's background saver. I like the way it helps my perspective to stand out and shine.

Let us all make a choice today, that we will do all we can to keep the light on in our lives. Let us all view life in the most thankful and grateful way. I promise that if you make a real effort to do this, that the sun will never set in your story and there will always be a happy ending!

IF
YOU
ARE
WAITING
FOR A SIGN
THIS
IS
IT.

Chapter 22

The White Butterfly

Send me a sign John that you are with me!

So much of who I am and what I do, goes back to the year my brother died. Though most may think that year was the hardest year of my life… it wasn't. Every year he is not with us is a challenge. Each time I get set back and struggle with my family or health is a challenge. In fact, the entire view of life is a challenge when the one person who understood you the most is missing.

John was and still is my best friend. If you asked my three other brothers how they feel about his loss, well… they would say the same. We may have each other to fall back on as siblings, but this team is always one player short in our game. We miss and adore John.

As a woman, my standard for men to live up to comes from all the incredible men who helped raise me. My father and brothers are the best of the best. I am so thankful for them helping me create a deep sense of strength and confidence in my being. It is why I was able to grow through a bad marriage, divorce, and find love again. You see, I had the best teachers. The best male friends anyone could ask for. Though today, I find myself aching for John's wisdom and advice. I am still trying to shape the woman I hope to be, and if John were here, I would be his priority.

Long time ago, over fifteen years now, I asked John to send me a sign. My family was so lost and broken after his death. My mother was a fragment of the woman who had raised me. She was lost in sorrow and anger. I knew when John died, she died too that day. I was faced with a challenge. To learn to let John go and to learn to keep him close all at the same time. I needed to grieve alone and grieve with the family. I needed to remind myself that everyone close to me was reborn in his death and I would have to find a way to get to know all these people all over again. My living brothers, my parents, and even myself. We were so different now. How could it be possible that one soul lost could change the entire dynamics of a family unit? I needed answers.

So one night, a long time ago, I sat at my computer and found what I was looking for. During the early months of John's passing, I was deep in the thick of planning my ten year high school reunion. I was also caring for my son, pregnant with my daughter Julia, and keeping my parents happy. The stress of life put a strain on my marriage and the emptiness I felt… the deep feeling of being all alone… consumed me. I begged John for a sign. Anything! He had come to visit me after his death and as a medium that is normal, but I needed more. I needed something to help bring his memory and our family back to life. I do not know why the thought popped in my head and who put it there, but white butterflies was all I could think about. I thought if John could just send us small white butterflies somehow we would know he was with us.

My mom asked me to read a special poem or write one for the anniversary of John's one year passing. Normally, that request would be met with ease, but not this time. I was lost. What to read. What to write. I just can't think anymore! So, I begged to the air around me and whoever might be listening to send me white butterflies.

The computer turned on before I could even touch a key. My email was open and I was already logged in which was odd. I had not been on the computer in months. I decided to scroll through all my missed messages. So many to delete and so much spam mail. I almost deleted one very important email, but the title in the subject section caught my attention. It read: "In memory of your brother." I was confused and didn't recognize the name of the sender. I sat quietly, opened the email, and took one last look around the room to see if my son Alex was awake. He was curled up on the couch asleep covered in a Winnie the Poo blanket.
The clock read 11:11 (a number that I associate to my deceased brother). I brought my attention back to the computer screen and began to read.

A woman who lived in Georgia (a complete stranger) had sent me the most perfect words. A poem. She explained she was an alumni of Locust Valley High School, like myself, but we had graduated Thirty years apart. She read on a reunion website that I was planning mine. Through an odd freak of nature, she came across news of my brother's passing. She too had once lost a sibling, and she felt compelled to send me an email.

I was so happy to receive her message and read on. She sent me a lovely poem, and I knew instantly that I would chose this one to read at my brother's memorial. I wrote her back immediately thanking her for the poem. We agreed to keep in touch.

I knew Alex was asleep but was so eager to print the poem. I set up the printer placing blue card stock paper in it. The paper was thick and heavy so I knew that the poem would look nice on it. I hit print and waited. As the paper emerged out of the printer I gasped. Tiny white butterflies were all over the blue paper surrounding these words:

> I will remember your smile along the way
> So bright and beautiful to start my day
> Stay ahead of the tears and sorrow
> Reach ahead to the comfort of tomorrow
> Give yourself time to heal
> Give yourself a moment to deal
> Remember your smile along the way
> Through stories, words, and when you pray
> Understand what life has given
> Hold your head high and keep on living
> No tears shall build your way
> Hold tight to each new day
> Remember your smile along the way
> Find peace in tomorrow and today.

Oh My God! White butterflies. I looked back at the poem on the screen yet saw nothing there. No butterflies. Just the words. I hit print again and waited. Nothing. The poem did print again, but no butterflies this time. What was going on here!

I immediately email the woman in Georgia. I asked why she had picked that poem and if it had butterflies on it when she sent it. Her email response was quick and it said:

"Hi Mary, it is Sharon. I am glad you liked the poem. I wrote it a long time ago. But there are no butterflies on it. Just the words I wrote. Why? Hope it helps you and makes you smile. Prayers and Love!"

I sat back in the chair and cried. Hours passed and I just continued to cry. John had answered me. I didn't need to see him or hear his voice. I just needed to pay attention and be patient for an answer to my request. He was listening. He always did and has proven himself over and over again throughout the years.

The butterfly symbol became this family's coping method. John was our butterfly. Over time, due to my own personal reasons and spiritual relationship with John, the Blue Butterfly symbol emerged. No matter what the color or how we get it, John is our sign of hope and transition. He is born into a new and beautiful life.

Today, nearing sixteen years gone, John still sends us butterflies and a variety of other symbols to look forward to. He finds a way to make his presence known each and every day. I cannot pretend that death does not hurt the ones left behind or will fade from our thoughts after years pass by. Grief is like the cycle of a day. There are bright moments and dark ones. When the next day emerges, so does our thoughts of the ones we love, miss, and honor.

I am not angry anymore that John lost his fight to cancer. I am realistic about the concepts of life and death. We all will pass one day. Some souls cross over young, while others live to see their skin wrinkle and pace slow from age. Life is a cycle too. So we must cherish our time here.

The butterfly is a beautiful creature. It begins its' life as a fragile larva inside a dark egg. As it grows, it emerges for the first time as a caterpillar – small and frail. After some time in its body delicate and soft, it builds a protective home to reflect and change. Our human shell is equal to the caterpillar. We move through life changing and growing from our experiences.

When it is time for our soul to transform, we emerge from our cocoon in our most beautiful essence. The Butterfly is us. The caterpillar never died, it became its higher self. It transitioned in order to fly and explore life in a new and delightful way. Our soul grows into death in order for us to find our wings and fly. It is our rebirth into an eternal life.

The words we speak and the actions that follow are going to shape and define us for the rest of our lives. We need to learn to grow healthy and transform into spirits that transmit love and respect to all those we encounter.

I often find myself searching the sky or browsing through gardens looking for butterflies. I am not just searching for the symbol that has helped me to heal all these years. I am searching for peace and love and most of all hope that life carries on in subtle gestures like my winged friend represents.

My wish for us all is to find our path in life. I see the beauty in everything… including death! There is nothing more perfect and humbling than knowing that there are greater forces outside our understanding that are working each day and night. They are committed to sending us big and small gestures to strengthen our hearts and heal our souls.

Maybe today begins a new day for us all, to not just receive gifts, but to go out in the world and deliver to one another promises of hope, compassion, and a bond of friendship that embraces all that life and death has created.

There is no greater gesture than the gift of love, kindness, and understanding.

Special Thanks

Julia Drew: Photography and Make-up Artistry
Follow Julia on Instagram: juliamaramakeup

A Look Ahead

Mary Drew is currently working on a collection of stories in hopes to share with you, the reader, many of her most memorable experiences as a Psychic Medium.

Feel free to reach out to Mary and inquire about private and group readings, events, fundraisers and more.

Thank you for taking this journey with Mary and honoring the memory of her brother John by purchasing this book.

Proceeds are continuously donated in John Scarola's name toward cancer research.

Blessings to all

Mary Drew – The North Shore Psychic Medium – Has been a resident of Long Island her entire life. Mary has been communicating with Spirits since the young age of ten. As a medium, Mary Drew has always used her empathic insight and kindness to deliver messages from departed souls to their loved ones.

Mary is the mother of four beautiful children and passionate about her rescued animals. She has always enjoyed spending time with her family and is committed to the health and wellness of her children.

Every life has a path to spiritual healing and happiness, and that journey drives Mary Drew to release her gift to the world. An established Medium, Mother, and now Author, Mary hopes to share her thoughts and experiences with those who have encountered grief, suffering and hardship.